NPT CODE

The Neural Protocol to Rewrite Reality from the Inside Out

The Hidden Architecture

What begins here doesn't end on paper.

Table of Contents

Introduction 7

Part I. The System Reset.. 15

Chapter 1: Deprogram the Loop.. 16

Chapter 2: Override the Internal Narrative 26

Part II. The Core Override 36

Chapter 3: Seal the Subconscious Gateway 38

Chapter 4: Interrupt the Default Pattern 50

Chapter 5: Command the Decision Layer 59

Part III. The Identity Installation 68

Chapter 6: Install the Identity Blueprint.............................. 70

Chapter 7: Activate the Influence Protocol 81

Chapter 8: Collapse the Old Self 92

Part IV. The Reality Rewrite 103

Chapter 9: Wire in Manifestation Triggers......................... 105

Chapter 10: Build the Perception Engine 115

Chapter 11: Master Internal State Control.......................... 126

Chapter 12: Lock the System 135

Introduction

Enter the System

You didn't find this book by chance.

Whatever loop you've been stuck in — overthinking, underperforming, self-doubt masked as logic, confidence that crumbles when tested — it didn't start with you. It was installed. Quietly. Over years. By repetition, emotional imprint, and the reinforcement of unconscious signals you never consciously agreed to.

And if it was installed, it can be rewritten.

The system you're about to enter is not a theory. It's a code. And like any code, it runs in the background — silently, invisibly, but with absolute control. Every decision you make, every word you speak, every belief you hold about what's possible or not, real or fake, strong or weak — all of it is governed by scripts you did not write. Some came from your parents, some from school, many from culture, and most from repetition. Not truth. Not choice. Repetition.

This book is the rewrite.

Not through willpower. Not through inspiration. Through installation.

The Loop You're In

Before we change anything, you need to understand where you're starting from.

Your mind is a system of patterns. Patterns that run until they're disrupted or overwritten. The way you react to criticism, the way you hesitate before speaking, the way you anticipate failure — these are not personality traits. They're **conditioned responses**, carved into your neural pathways by repeated inputs.

And here's what matters: the loop doesn't care whether the inputs were true or false. Your brain isn't loyal to truth. It's loyal to repetition. It locks onto whatever pattern is repeated most — not what's right, or healthy, or powerful. Just what's familiar.

This is why you can *know* you're worthy, but still feel inadequate. Why you can *read* about success but still sabotage every opportunity. You're trying to use conscious logic to override subconscious code. That never works. Not sustainably.

Reprogramming requires access to the subconscious — and the subconscious speaks in emotion, identity, and pattern. Not logic. Not words. Code.

This book will not give you more information. It will give you **a system to run**. A protocol designed to break the existing loops and install new ones.

The Code is the Practice

Every part of this program introduces a new directive — a specific neural pattern to disrupt or install. You won't be reflecting on ideas. You'll be running code.

This is why execution is everything. You can't just read the words. You must act. Speak the phrase. Break the habit. Run the ritual. Override the thought. Only action rewires.

And don't expect emotional comfort. Change doesn't feel good at first. Rewiring doesn't feel like motivation. It feels like resistance. Friction. Disorientation. That's how you know it's working.

The system does not require belief. It requires action.

You don't have to believe you're powerful. You just have to act as if you are. Belief will follow. That's how the subconscious works. It doesn't listen to what you say. It listens to what you repeat, embody, and reinforce.

If you follow the system without skipping, without diluting, without negotiating — your perception, your internal programming, and your outcomes will shift.

We're not going to explain every detail of how it works. That's not how this book operates. You're not here to study it. You're here to install it.

You'll soon discover what NPT truly means. Some say Neural Pattern Transmutation. Others call it a Non-Permitted Technology. The truth is, it's not what you call it — it's what it does to you.

Now step in.

The subconscious is not rational. It is reactive, fast, and pattern-based. It doesn't care if your pattern is destructive. It cares only that the pattern is

8

predictable. This is why change feels like danger. Because to the deep mind, unfamiliar equals unsafe.

The NPT system is built to use that against itself.

Each directive you'll follow in this protocol has a specific function: some are designed to destabilize faulty loops, others to replace them with new commands, others to anchor those commands through action, sensation, or disruption. You're not just shifting thoughts. You're shifting access. You're creating new neural sequences, and when repeated through intention and structure, those sequences begin to fire automatically. Once that happens, what used to be forced becomes natural.

That's what real rewiring is.

Most people get stuck in a loop not because they enjoy it, but because they don't know how to exit. Their conscious desires are hijacked by unconscious scripts. This system is a map out. Not through motivation. Through construction. Day by day, phrase by phrase, loop by loop.

This process is internal first, but it is not passive. You will speak aloud. You will confront resistance. You will run rituals that feel strange or intense. You may feel exposed. That's the access point. That's the place in the mind where conditioning lives — and where it can be rewritten.

Every element of the system is intentional. Even the order. Some days are designed to push. Others to seal. Others to install a state that you haven't embodied in years — or ever. The structure matters. Trust it.

There will be a moment when it clicks. A subtle shift. You'll notice a familiar trigger, but your response will be different. You won't hesitate where you used to. You'll speak where you used to silence. You'll feel space where there used to be urgency or noise. This is not a dramatic explosion. It is a silent override. That's how power returns. Quietly. Irreversibly.

You are not broken. You're coded. And you're about to become the one who writes the code.

You won't need to understand every neural theory behind the rituals to benefit from them. But in many cases, you'll feel the science inside the practice. There's intention behind every pattern disruptor and every installation phrase. Behind every gesture, breath, or visualization. These are tools derived from fields you won't find in mainstream self-help — they come from studies on memory reconsolidation, identity plasticity, reticular bias training, language reframing, and trauma loop destabilization. You're not being asked to believe in any of it. You're being asked to run it.

Read each directive once. Then read it again slower. Speak it aloud if the protocol tells you to. Don't analyze it. Don't soften it. Don't skip parts. Skipping parts is the old code talking. Let it die.

Your only goal is to complete one part at a time. Nothing more.

The language in this book may feel different. It's supposed to. It's not written for your comfort. It's written for your reconstruction. You may notice sharp phrasing, short commands, or unusual instructions. Don't dilute them. If you feel resistance, that's the subconscious trying to protect the loop. That's when you push. That's when it changes.

You will not be the same person by the end of this system. If you are, you didn't run it.

Begin now. Day one is waiting.

System online. Code initializing. Execute.

What NPT Really Does to the Mind

You've been taught to think of your mind as something static. Like a personality, fixed and unchangeable. But what you call your "mind" is really a set of responses — scripts that fire without your permission. Your reactions, beliefs, habits, emotional reflexes, even your self-image — they're all code. Not character.

NPT doesn't "motivate" the mind. It rewrites it.

Not by force. Not by positive thinking. By systematically triggering neural rewiring through targeted disruption, conscious override, and subconscious installation. In other words, this isn't therapy. This is engineering.

To understand what this protocol does, you need to first know what you're working with. The brain is plastic. That's not a metaphor. It means that the way it's wired — the patterns it runs, the associations it builds, the habits it reinforces — can be broken and rebuilt. This is called neuroplasticity, and it's not new. But the problem is, most people engage neuroplasticity passively. You absorb patterns without meaning to. NPT flips that dynamic. It gives you control over the patterns you're building, down to the layer where identity lives.

That layer is not verbal. It's not analytical. It lives in image, repetition, sensation, and emotion. That's why affirmations without feeling don't work. That's why knowledge without friction doesn't change anything. You don't change through information. You change through **instruction paired with intensity**.

That's the layer NPT works in.

This system is structured around what you might call neural leverage — getting maximum change through small, intentional disruptions repeated with precision. You'll speak short commands out loud. You'll create mental tension. You'll anchor phrases to actions. You'll break a pattern not by analyzing it, but by doing something that contradicts it physically or verbally. These actions may seem simple, even strange. That's on purpose. Simplicity is what makes a command installable. It's not the complexity of the action that changes your mind. It's the consistency with which you do it, and the intensity of emotional engagement when you do. That's how the brain decides what's real and worth repeating. Not based on logic. Based on imprint.

NPT uses this mechanism to your advantage. Instead of letting fear or doubt imprint on your system, you'll create controlled disruptions — micro-overrides — that act like injections of new code. Some of them will feel subtle. Others will feel confrontational. All of them will bypass the conscious filters your mind usually hides behind.

You're not going to fix yourself with this protocol. You're going to **install a new self**.

And that requires getting under the surface. The system doesn't care what you *believe* about yourself. It cares what you *repeat*. So if you repeat weakness, the system locks it in. If you repeat power — even before you believe it — the system will begin to accept it as the new operating norm.

Most people try to wait until they believe something before they act on it. That's backwards. The brain doesn't work like that. You act first. Then the brain builds the belief around the action. This is why your identity has felt stuck. You've been waiting to feel ready. You've been hoping that clarity or confidence will arrive before you move. But clarity is built through forward motion. Confidence is built through conflict. Not comfort.

The NPT system places you in controlled mental conflict — enough to trigger rewiring, never enough to destabilize you. Each step is built to stretch your current identity boundary. And once that boundary stretches, it doesn't return to its original shape.

You don't bounce back. You upgrade forward.

Your old programming survives by going unnoticed. It hides in the normal. That's why NPT doesn't just bring awareness — it introduces interruption. It inserts friction where you've been running smooth but destructive scripts. It brings you into contact with the automated reflexes you usually bypass. That contact point is everything. It creates what your mind interprets as instability. And in that instability, new wiring becomes possible.

This system also uses timing. Certain actions, when taken at precise emotional or mental peaks, go deeper than they would otherwise. If you've ever had a moment where one sentence hit you like lightning — not because it was new, but because you were finally open — then you already understand how timing governs depth. NPT protocols are built to create that opening, then install the new pattern immediately.

This is also why small rituals are powerful. The mind does not distinguish between symbolic action and literal consequence. If you stand taller and speak with force, the brain assumes you are in control. If you break a pattern out loud — even if no one else hears you — the brain assumes something real just shifted. When you repeat this, the assumption becomes structure.

Over time, the system stops reacting as it did. The same trigger no longer produces the same loop. You create a gap. A pause. In that pause, choice enters. And with repeated use of that choice, identity reshapes itself.

You are not trying to become someone new. You are becoming someone more precise.

Precision is power. And that's what most mental systems lack. They offer insight, but not targeting. They give you ideas, but no architecture. NPT gives you daily neural targeting. You don't change your life by vaguely "feeling better." You change it by altering your internal commands at the micro level, one layer at a time, until new decisions become reflex.

These decisions compound. They adjust the tone of your voice, the sharpness of your perception, the tension in your body, the speed of your reactions. Others begin to notice it before you do. Not because you've explained it. But because the energy signal has changed. You're not operating from the same frame anymore. And whether someone understands that or not, they feel it.

This isn't just mental. It's social. Psychological. Relational. You'll feel it when you speak and people listen. When you walk into a space and the dynamic shifts. That's not magic. That's programming. Internal changes ripple outward. They alter tone, posture, rhythm, decisions — everything. That's what NPT is designed for.

It is not a philosophy. It is not a mindset. It is a structured override. It works because it doesn't rely on your mood. It works when you're tired. It works when you're doubting. It works when you want to quit. Because it runs on **execution**, not emotion.

This is what most people miss. They think the mind needs fixing before the system can run. The truth is, the system runs first. The mind follows. You are not optimizing a broken machine. You are uploading new instructions to a powerful one that was hijacked by repetition.

Once you understand that, everything becomes clear. You don't have to get it perfect. You just have to get it running. Every ritual, every command, every micro-disruption is one less loop for the old code to hold onto. Eventually, it stops fighting. The identity shift finalizes.

That's what NPT really does to the mind.

It deletes permission. It grants override.

And once override is active, the entire system bends. Not to what you hope for. To what you command.

Part I. The System Reset

Before you install anything new, you have to break what's running now.

Part I is not about improvement. It's about interruption. Your current operating system is built from repetition, not truth. These first chapters are designed to expose it — not by talking about it, but by pulling you into direct confrontation with the automatic loops you've never questioned. The hesitation before action. The internal voice that rewrites your value before you speak. The resistance that shows up when opportunity does. That's the code we're targeting now.

The System Reset phase works by destabilizing your baseline patterns. Most self-help teaches you how to build over them. This protocol breaks them. It introduces calculated friction, forces short-term disorientation, and begins the neurological process of pattern collapse. This is what real change feels like. Not clarity. Not motivation. Disruption.

You may feel resistance. Good. You may feel doubt. Good. You may want to skip or soften the work. That means you're exactly where the old program wants you to stop.

Each chapter in this section is a weapon. A tool to identify and override default programming. You'll learn how to recognize the loop in real time. How to strip power from your old internal narrative. How to shut down external influence at the sensory level. And how to begin inserting counter-commands into the subconscious where identity actually forms.

You're not here to discuss transformation. You're here to run it. And that begins with disassembly.

Every day you execute a directive, you are no longer just reacting to your programming. You're rewriting it.

Welcome to reset. Run the first line.

Chapter 1: Deprogram the Loop

The Invisible Script You've Been Running

There is a voice inside you that sounds like your own. But it isn't. It's older. Older than your current thoughts. Older than your goals. It's the voice of the script — the one you didn't write, but have been following for years without knowing it.

This script governs more than you think. It shapes how you move through the world, how you speak to yourself, how you filter feedback, and how you interpret possibility. It's not loud. It doesn't argue. It just runs. Quietly. Predictably. Invisibly.

And that's the danger.

The script began forming the moment your nervous system started associating repetition with safety. Every reaction you saw modeled, every reward or punishment you received, every moment of praise or rejection — all of it fed lines into the code. Eventually, your system locked them in. Not because they were right. But because they were consistent.

Your mind learned that familiarity equals survival. Even if the pattern was self-destructive. Even if it limited your voice, your reach, or your self-concept. If it repeated, it installed. If it installed, it became the script. And the script became you.

But here's the truth: the voice you think is "you" — the doubt before speaking, the pause before action, the subtle anxiety when things start going right — that voice was installed. It isn't native. It's not your essence. It's code you absorbed.

Which means it can be broken.

This chapter is not about identifying every belief you hold. That would waste time. The script doesn't care about your conscious beliefs. It runs beneath them. You could believe in success and still sabotage it. You could believe in your power and still hesitate when it matters. The script overrides belief.

It's written in reflex.

To break it, you don't need to understand every line. You just need to recognize its presence. How? By noticing where your reactions do not match your desires. Where your words contradict your outcomes. Where your habits keep pulling you back into the same emotional baseline, no matter what you try to build on top of it.

The script shows up in the gap between what you say you want and what you unconsciously allow yourself to receive. It shows up in that moment where you almost speak — and don't. Where you almost commit — and don't. Where you feel energy, then sabotage it before it grows.

These are not random glitches. They are checkpoints. The system is trying to run the old code. It doesn't care what you want. It cares what has been rehearsed.

This is why you've been stuck. You've tried to shift behavior with force instead of rewiring the pattern that drives it. You've tried to override the output without touching the script itself. That approach will always collapse. Because the code reasserts itself the moment pressure hits.

The NPT protocol doesn't teach you to resist the script. It teaches you to overwrite it. Not by arguing with your thoughts. Not by journaling them to death. By replacing the code through controlled disruption, spoken command, and identity contradiction.

But first, you have to locate the script while it's running. Not after. Not in reflection. In real time.

This begins with recognition. You'll need to track your reactions like they're not yours. Because they aren't. Not yet. You'll learn to treat your internal voice as a system process — not a source of truth, not a personality trait, but a line of code. And like any code, it becomes visible when it malfunctions.

That's the entry point.

Start to notice the moments that feel automatic. Not just in behavior, but in emotion. That flush of shame when you speak up. That drop in energy when you start something new. The tension in your chest when things are going well. These aren't just feelings. They're signals that the script is running.

You don't need to fix these reactions in the moment. You only need to observe them with detachment, like you're tracking a pattern in someone else. The goal isn't judgment. It's data. When you feel hesitation, delay, deflection, or self-doubt, identify it for what it is: a prewritten response. One that served a function in the past, but no longer does.

The script runs on familiarity. Every time you react the same way to a familiar input, the script strengthens. This is why "trying harder" often reinforces the problem. The mind interprets your effort as evidence that the script is needed. That tension becomes confirmation. And so the code deepens.

You break that loop not with willpower, but with contradiction.

The NPT system will begin introducing counter-loops. You'll be instructed to speak or move in ways that directly oppose your usual pattern. You might be asked to hold eye contact longer than you're used to. To speak a phrase that feels too bold. To act with speed where you usually hesitate. These actions are not random. They're code injections. The goal is to interrupt the neural groove the old script runs through.

Repetition is what created the loop. Precision disruption is what breaks it.

Once you start interrupting the pattern enough times, the brain begins to open a new path. It doesn't delete the old one — it just weakens it. And with enough friction, it loses its default status. That's the shift. Not total deletion. Displacement.

This shift can't happen through understanding alone. You can study psychology for ten years and still run the same script. You can talk about your childhood patterns for hours and still flinch when it's time to lead. Knowledge is not access. Only action rewires.

This is why the daily directives matter. Each one is designed to bring you into a live moment of choice. Do I run the script, or do I override? That decision, repeated again and again, is what builds the new baseline.

You may be tempted to think the shift needs to be dramatic. That you need a total personality transformation to count it as success. That's false. Real change is subtle. Often invisible from the outside at first. It looks like silence where there used to be overexplanation. It looks like holding your posture instead of collapsing into apology. It looks like taking a risk without announcing it.

What matters is that you start seeing the script from the outside. Once you do, you're no longer inside its authority. You may still feel it, but you won't follow it without question. That's the beginning of sovereignty. The moment you stop mistaking old programming for identity.

It's not enough to know the script exists. You must learn to confront it mid-sentence. To name it when it tries to run. To speak a new line in its place — even if your voice shakes. Especially then.

This is the skill: recognition without collapse. Observation without compliance. That's how the script weakens. Not by analyzing it endlessly, but by outliving it with new action.

You were not born with this code. You inherited it. And starting now, you begin the process of releasing it. One override at a time.

Identify and Interrupt the Repeating Thought Chains

Your mind doesn't think in isolation. It thinks in chains. One thought leads to another, which triggers an emotion, which triggers another thought, and so on. These chains are fast. Faster than your awareness. You rarely notice when they start. You only notice how they end — in hesitation, distraction, anxiety, overthinking, or paralysis.

The chain doesn't need to be long. One cue is enough. A glance. A word. A tone of voice. Suddenly, the mind begins pulling memories, associations, worst-case scenarios, imagined reactions. Within seconds, you're reacting to a reality that doesn't exist — except inside your system.

This is how most people live. Not from present input, but from mental chains triggered by the past and reinforced by fear. They don't see what's happening. They only feel drained. Disoriented. Scattered. And they call that normal.

NPT treats these chains as systems. Loops that run without permission. And like any system, they can be disrupted. But only if you can see them in motion.

The first step is recognition. Most repeating thought chains begin the same way — with a pattern-specific opening line. It might sound like a question. *"What if I fail?"* It might be a judgment. *"I never get this right."* It might be a memory, seemingly random but charged. Whatever form it takes, it's almost always subtle. It feels familiar. Not dangerous.

And that's the trap. The chain disguises itself as reflection or preparation. But it's not preparing you. It's delaying you. It's disempowering you in real time. The longer you run it, the more it reinforces its position as the default path.

That's why interruption must come early.

You won't always catch it at the first word. That's fine. You don't need perfect awareness. You just need *timely* awareness. When you notice that the chain is active, name it. Not with judgment. With precision. Say, *"This is not thinking. This is looping."*

That phrase matters. It separates you from the process. It reframes the chain as a pattern, not as truth. And once you separate from it, you can disrupt it. Disruption is not about finding a positive thought to replace the negative one. That's ineffective. It gives the loop more attention. The goal isn't to argue with the chain. The goal is to *break it*.

20

There are three reliable ways to break a chain: contradiction, shock, or movement. You'll learn to apply each throughout the NPT protocol. In this phase, we focus on contradiction.

Contradiction means inserting a thought, phrase, or action that directly opposes the pattern the chain is trying to run. If the loop starts with fear, you speak certainty. If it starts with delay, you move immediately. If it starts with self-doubt, you speak a phrase that feels above your current self-concept. Not because you believe it yet — but because the shock of it interrupts the expected progression.

This is not affirmation. This is override.

Affirmations are passive. Overrides are disruptive. They feel intrusive on purpose. That's how they work. The brain is pattern-oriented. When you interrupt a pattern with something incompatible, the sequence breaks. And in that break, you have a window. A few seconds of mental stillness before the system tries to reboot.

What you do in that window is critical. That's when you insert the new command. Not later. Not after reflection. Immediately.

The override phrase you use doesn't need to be profound. It needs to be disruptive. What matters is not the elegance of the words, but the intensity with which they cut across the loop. If your chain says, *"This is too much,"* you say, *"I run this."* If it says, *"What if they reject me?"* you say, *"I decide the frame."* These phrases don't need to feel comfortable. They need to feel sharp. The discomfort means they're working.

Most of your mental chains rely on emotional familiarity. They repeat because they create a predictable internal state. The outcome doesn't matter. What matters is that the emotion is known. That's why negative chains survive. Not because they feel good, but because they feel familiar. And the brain, in absence of conscious override, chooses familiar every time.

By interrupting that pattern, you force the system to process uncertainty. This is uncomfortable. That discomfort is not a warning sign. It's a marker of transition. The brain has been pulled off its automatic path. The chain has been broken. And in that space, identity can shift.

You will not stop all chains forever. That's not the goal. The goal is to stop reacting to them as if they're real. Once you can observe the loop as a system instead of engaging with it as reality, you no longer feed it. Starved of your emotional compliance, the loop weakens. With practice, it stops even trying to run.

This shift happens faster than most people think. Not because the brain is easy to change, but because it is built to adapt. The problem has never been your capacity. It's been your repetition. NPT gives you new repetitions. Repetition is not the enemy. It's the tool. You just have to turn it on the right target.

This is why every directive you'll follow includes some form of interruption. You won't just be observing patterns. You'll be intervening in them. In real time. You'll be breaking the sequence before it reaches full charge. This matters. Because the longer the chain runs, the harder it is to override. Emotion builds momentum. Thought becomes chemistry. And chemistry becomes behavior.

You must catch it upstream.

This is the discipline: to act quickly, not perfectly. The script will always invite you to delay. To think it through. To wait for a better moment. That's the trap. You break the chain by responding with speed, not refinement. You speak the override phrase before you think it's working. You shift your posture before your confidence kicks in. You contradict the pattern before your mind approves.

That's what real interruption feels like. It's not polished. It's jagged. It cuts through the noise because it refuses to ask permission.

You are training your system to respond to new input as if it's already familiar. That's how a new loop takes hold. The mind doesn't check for truth. It checks for repetition. Your job is not to explain the override. Your job is to run it often enough that the system stops questioning it.

Eventually, the chain stops triggering. Not because you outsmarted it. Because it no longer recognizes you. The pattern was built for a version of you that no longer exists. Once that version is overwritten, the old response has nowhere to land.

This is how the mind bends. Not by force. By reprogramming the sequence it expects to follow. The moment you break that expectation, you gain access to a new command line.

And once you're there, you don't negotiate with the chain. You replace it. Instantly. Repeatedly. Until it forgets it ever had control.

Neural Disruption: How to Break the Loop in Real Time

The most dangerous thing about mental loops is that they don't ask for your permission. They run before you notice them, and by the time you do, they've already shaped your posture, your emotion, your energy, and your self-perception.

This is why most mindset advice fails. It's always delivered too late. You're told to reframe, to calm down, to think differently — but the loop is already active. It's not asking you to think. It's pulling you into compliance. That's not a psychological problem. It's a neural one.

Loops are electrical. They're fast. And once they reach a certain charge, they override logic and trigger the body. You go from thought to state. State becomes behavior. And by the time it's over, you're left wondering how you got there again.

You don't fix this by becoming more reflective. You fix it by becoming more precise. And precision starts with disruption.

Neural disruption means introducing a pattern your system doesn't expect. A movement, a phrase, a breath, a gesture — something that contradicts the loop so completely that the brain has to pause. This pause is not just mental. It's physical. The pattern is interrupted at the synaptic level. Circuits that were about to fire are suddenly halted. In that break, you gain access. You can insert a new command, shift your internal state, or exit the loop entirely.

The key is that it must happen in real time.

You can't wait until the loop is over. You have to catch it while it's happening, while your body is leaning in, while your mind is beginning to spiral. That's the window. It's small. But it's enough.

Disruption works because the brain is predictive. It's not just responding to the present. It's constantly forecasting. Based on the past, it predicts how you'll react to this moment. And it prepares accordingly. It sets the emotional tone, primes your posture, adjusts your voice, locks in assumptions. This prediction becomes the path. The longer it runs uninterrupted, the stronger it becomes.

Disruption breaks the prediction.

You act in a way that contradicts what the brain expected. You speak when you were about to freeze. You slow your breathing when you were about to panic. You move forward when the system anticipated hesitation. This shock creates friction. And friction is the beginning of plasticity.

You don't need to understand every mechanism behind it. But you do need to execute it on command.

This is why every loop-breaking ritual in this system is short. You don't need a long process. You need a fast, repeatable trigger. One that works even when the loop is already starting to run.

To use disruption effectively, you need to first know your signal — the internal marker that a loop is activating. It could be a drop in energy, a shift in body language, a tightening in the chest, a sensation of pulling back. This signal is unique to you. Your job is to identify it, so you can act on it fast.

Once the signal shows up, you don't argue with it. You don't ask why it's there. You insert the disruption. Immediately.

The faster you act, the more powerful the disruption becomes. You're not giving the loop time to reinforce itself. You're not analyzing or negotiating. You're breaking the sequence at the speed of awareness. That speed matters. The longer you hesitate, the more control the pattern regains.

It doesn't have to be dramatic. Subtle but deliberate action is enough. The shift might be physical — clenching your fist, adjusting your stance, exhaling forcefully through the nose. It might be vocal — a sharp override phrase spoken aloud with intention. It might be visual — locking your gaze forward instead of down. These are not random tricks. They're controlled inputs sent to your nervous system to signal a new response.

Your brain is always waiting for instruction. If you don't give it one, it runs the last pattern by default. Disruption is the insertion of a new instruction at the moment of choice.

You are not doing this to feel better. You are doing it to rewire faster. Sometimes you'll feel resistance. The urge to delay or downplay the need to act will try to disguise itself as logic. That urge is the loop defending itself. It thrives on subtlety. If it can convince you to wait five more seconds, it has already won.

Precision overrides that defense. You interrupt at the first signal. Even if your heart rate jumps. Even if your voice shakes. Especially then. You don't wait for confidence. You move and let the mind recalibrate after.

This is the core of real-time rewiring. Your internal experience doesn't have to be clean. It just has to be *interrupted* with action that contradicts the expected path. When you do this enough times, the mind stops assuming the old loop is your preference. It stops protecting it. It begins routing energy through the new path.

That's how patterns die. Not by logic. By neglect.

The brain prunes unused neural paths. If you stop reinforcing the old loop and start feeding the new one, it rewires itself. You don't need to force it. You need to stop feeding the script and start feeding the override. The results will follow biology.

The mistake most people make is trying to intellectualize their way out of a loop. They want to understand the root cause, trace the timeline, make sense of the emotion. That might feel satisfying in the short term, but it rarely changes the pattern. Because you're still running it. You're just analyzing it as it controls your system.

NPT doesn't ask you to understand every root. It asks you to break the chain where it matters most — where the loop becomes action. This is the tipping point. That's where leverage exists. Not before. Not after. Right there.

Once you've disrupted the loop, don't pause to celebrate. Seal the moment. Give your system a closing signal. That could be a phrase, a breath, a snap, or a step forward. Something that tells the brain: new pattern completed. The more you reinforce this, the more automatic it becomes. Over time, your new default becomes the very disruption you had to force at the beginning.

This is what it means to rewire in real time. Not by removing the loop. By refusing to serve it. Not by waiting to feel ready. By moving faster than the system expects. And not by hoping you change. By commanding it.

This is not about perfection. It's about authority.

The loop may still try to speak. But it won't run the show anymore. Because you'll be the one giving the orders.

Chapter 2: Override the Internal Narrative

The Voice Inside Isn't You

Most people have never questioned the voice in their head. They assume it's theirs. That it represents truth, logic, or intuition. That it's guiding them with accuracy. But what if it isn't?

What if that voice isn't yours at all?

What if it was assembled over time, piece by piece, from every instruction, rejection, and observation you absorbed in childhood? What if it sounds like you because your nervous system wrapped it in your tone, but the content was never yours to begin with?

The internal voice you hear when you fail, hesitate, or plan — the one narrating your worth, your risk, your value, your future — that voice is mostly a construction. A blend of voices you learned to obey. And while it may now wear your accent and your cadence, its script was written by others.

This doesn't mean the voice is always wrong. It means it was never examined. And unexamined internal dialogue becomes law.

You don't need to have experienced trauma to carry this. All it takes is repetition. A father's tone when you didn't get something right. A teacher's silence after you spoke. A moment of embarrassment your body never fully forgot. The nervous system records those experiences without consulting your conscious mind. And it doesn't store them as isolated memories. It turns them into generalized responses. Which means the next time you face something unfamiliar or high-stakes, the voice fires automatically.

It tells you to be careful. To hold back. To stay small. To wait. And because the voice sounds internal, you believe it's intuitive.

But it's not.

It's reactive. And its job isn't to make you powerful. Its job is to keep you consistent.

Consistency equals safety in the subconscious mind. Even if that consistency keeps you stuck. The internal voice doesn't care about your potential. It cares about not being shocked. It wants you to repeat what's known, even if what's known is ineffective, exhausting, or false.

This is how so many people remain trapped in mental loops. They think they're being cautious, balanced, or wise — but what's actually happening is that the voice is pulling them back to the emotional settings it knows best. The settings you were conditioned into. The ones that got practiced the most.

You'll notice this voice most clearly when you try to stretch.

When you speak more directly than usual. When you take on more responsibility. When you decide to move faster, command more space, or trust your instinct without explaining it. The voice will show up with all its practiced authority. Not with shouting, but with quiet suggestion. Doubt dressed as logic. Hesitation dressed as maturity.

That's the trap. The voice doesn't sound like resistance. It sounds like strategy. Like reflection. Like protecting you from mistakes.

But if you listen closely, you'll hear what it's actually doing: recycling the past into the present. Protecting you from risks that no longer exist. Filtering your power through old fears that were never yours to begin with.

The only reason the voice seems trustworthy is because it has been rehearsed more than any other. It's not the most accurate, just the most familiar. And familiarity feels safe — even when it isn't.

But here's what changes everything: the moment you hear the voice as separate from who you really are, you gain power over it. This recognition doesn't mean the voice disappears. It means you're no longer hypnotized by it.

Most people stay stuck because they try to overpower the voice or silence it. But suppression only reinforces its presence. It becomes louder, more cunning. What works instead is observation without attachment. The ability to hear it and *not* obey.

This is where your rewiring begins.

Not with a fight, but with awareness. You watch the voice fire its script — and you choose not to run it. You feel the familiar pull to shrink, delay, or doubt — and instead of reacting, you hold the line. You don't need to replace it with another voice yet. You just need to break the trance.

At first, this will feel strange. Like walking barefoot after years in shoes. You'll feel exposed, unsure. That's not a sign of failure. That's the sign that you're in new territory — and your nervous system hasn't mapped it yet.

This is exactly where NPT comes in. The method doesn't eliminate the internal voice. It disrupts the automatic agreement with it. It gives you the tools to challenge what was once automatic. It creates new neural scaffolding, so that over time, different internal scripts become more natural, more frequent, and eventually — more dominant.

The goal isn't to become a person who never hears doubt. The goal is to become someone who doesn't serve it.

You start creating space between the voice and the command. You begin questioning, even when the voice feels true. And with every moment of separation, your system registers something profound: safety does not require obedience to that voice anymore.

This realization is subtle, but powerful. It's the foundation for actual reprogramming. Because until you decouple identity from that voice, every new habit or affirmation you try will sit on top of an unexamined foundation.

This is why most mindset work doesn't hold. It tries to install new thoughts without auditing the old narrator.

Once you identify the voice as *a* voice — not *your* voice — you begin the process of choosing. Not reacting. Not defending. Just choosing. With presence.

In time, a deeper voice begins to surface. One that is not reactive. One that doesn't speak in fear, pattern, or old reward-punishment frames. It's quieter at first, because it's newer. But it's real. And it's yours.

That voice doesn't rush. It doesn't protect. It doesn't run scripts. It speaks only when you're clear enough to hear it. And when you do, you'll recognize it — not by the words it uses, but by the way your entire system settles.

You'll feel the difference.

The inner noise will still be there, but it will no longer own your decisions. That's when you know you've shifted. That's when you're no longer living from the loop, but from awareness.

That's when the voice inside stops being the master — and becomes just another echo you've outgrown.

Installing a New Dominant Identity

Once you break free from the default loop, the next question becomes: what replaces it?

Nature hates a vacuum. So does your subconscious. If you remove the old programming but leave the space empty, the mind will revert to what it knows — even if what it knows is painful or limiting. That's why disruption alone is not enough. Disruption clears the ground, but identity is what anchors the shift.

Every thought you repeat, every emotion you feed, every decision you make — these are not just behaviors. They are signals to your subconscious, confirming who you believe yourself to be. You're not just doing things. You're becoming someone.

That "someone" isn't formed once and for all. It is sculpted over time, through repetition and emotional intensity. You've already done this — unconsciously — in the past. What we're doing now is taking control of the sculptor's hand.

To create a new dominant identity, you don't start by pretending to be someone else. You start by defining, in absolute clarity, who the dominant version of you actually is. Not the aspirational fantasy. The true aligned archetype. The one that has always been there, just buried beneath noise and conditioning.

This isn't about faking confidence or forcing positivity. It's about choosing the signal you want your nervous system to amplify. If your current identity is built around survival, avoidance, or fear, then every action you take will pass through that filter. You can't override that filter by willpower alone. That's why we install a new one.

Installing doesn't mean chanting mantras or repeating "I am powerful" until it feels real. Those tricks don't last. Instead, installation happens through consistency, emotional congruence, and nervous system alignment. The new identity must be chosen, felt, and *acted on* — even before it feels like it fits.

This process is uncomfortable. It will feel inauthentic at first. That's not a sign of failure. It's a sign of friction between the old neural circuit and the new one you're building. Friction is the heat of rewiring.

To install the new dominant identity, we begin by making it real in the mind — but not just through visualization. Through *decision*.

Visualization without decision is fantasy. But when you decide that this identity is now your operating system, your choices begin to shift. You notice the gap between the behavior of the old you and the one you're stepping into. That awareness creates tension. And tension creates transformation.

Once the decision is made, you must embed it through *evidence*. The subconscious doesn't trust words. It trusts patterns. The brain maps identity through action and emotional charge. That means every time you act in alignment with your new identity — even in micro-ways — you're reinforcing it.

The mistake most people make is waiting to *feel* like the new identity before behaving as if it were already installed. That's backwards. Identity responds to what you *do*, not what you hope to become. When your nervous system sees repeated action that reflects power, clarity, and decisiveness, it recalibrates its baseline.

Even small shifts count, but they must be done with precision. For example, if your new identity is deeply intentional and doesn't waste energy on distractions, then the moment you catch yourself spiraling into a thought loop or aimless scrolling, you must intervene. Not with guilt. With correction. That instant interruption followed by redirection is what teaches your system that the old behavior is no longer the command structure.

You are reconditioning your baseline reactions. You're telling your brain, "This is not who I am anymore," and then showing it who you actually are — not through affirmations, but through embodied response. That's why repetition is essential. Without it, the brain reverts to its most efficient pathway, which is almost always the old one.

But repetition alone is not enough. Intensity matters.

Emotional charge is what locks in new wiring. When you move with presence, when you feel the discomfort of acting beyond your usual self-image and *still* take the action, that emotional intensity accelerates the installation. You can't fake this part. It has to be real. And it often is, because becoming someone new requires internal risk. That risk brings fear. And if you use the fear as fuel, it becomes the fire that forges the shift.

The more emotionally real the moment is, the deeper the identity embeds.

Over time, you'll notice that old impulses become weaker. The hesitation to speak your truth fades. The tendency to default to victim-mode shrinks. The clarity you once had to summon becomes your new default. These are signs that your dominant identity has shifted from concept to reality.

Still, there will be days when the old patterns knock louder. Stress, fatigue, or external pressure can trigger fallback responses. That doesn't mean the new identity has failed. It means the old one has sensed a window of return. Your job isn't to punish yourself for slipping. Your job is to recover faster, with less emotional charge, and to re-enter the new operating system with full intent.

This is where tracking matters.

Track your choices. Track your self-talk. Track your reactions under pressure. Not obsessively, but consciously. You're not just building a new identity — you're building trust in it. And trust comes from seeing it hold up under tension.

The real power of this process isn't just internal. The world starts responding differently to you. People mirror back new forms of respect, attraction, or resistance — depending on who you've become. New opportunities feel magnetized. Not because reality changed, but because your perception filter has shifted. You now notice what aligns with your dominant identity and ignore what doesn't.

That's how reality begins to bend. Not through wishful thinking, but through internal coherence. When who you are, what you believe, and how you behave are unified, your external results stop feeling random.

They become inevitable.

The Language of Power and Mental Imprinting

Language isn't just how we communicate. It's how we program. Every word you speak, think, or absorb carries more than meaning — it carries command. In the world of neural pattern transmutation, language is not descriptive. It is *directive*. And most people have been running unconscious scripts for years without realizing that those scripts are precisely why they remain stuck.

Powerful language doesn't mean loud or aggressive. It means aligned. Precise. Pattern-breaking. To speak with power is to speak with *intention that imprints*. This is where most people fail — not in desire, but in the default language that weakens the signal of that desire at the level of the subconscious.

When someone says, "I'll try," what the mind hears is: "I'm not certain." When they say, "Hopefully it works out," the subconscious receives the message: "I don't expect this to happen." These aren't just innocent phrases. They are micro-imprints that define the edge of what your brain believes is possible or permitted.

The subconscious mind takes repetition as reality. That's why people who constantly reinforce doubt, hesitation, or disempowerment — even in casual speech — find themselves living out exactly what they say. This is not magic. This is cognitive conditioning. You are *imprinting* through your language. And every imprint reinforces a behavioral track.

Let's get specific.

If your goal is to rewire your dominant patterns and rewrite your identity, your internal and external language must align with that identity. There is no bypass here. You cannot speak like the old version of yourself and expect the new one to emerge. You must adopt the language of power not as a performance, but as a *practice of recalibration*.

This includes how you speak to yourself in moments of uncertainty. It includes the tone you use when you describe your goals. It includes the framing you use when talking about your past. Every time you say "I always screw this up," or "This is just who I am," you are reaffirming the very script you're trying to escape.

So, what is the language of power?

It is language that embeds *certainty*, *command*, and *coherence*. It eliminates weak modifiers and vague intentions. It doesn't entertain unnecessary hypotheticals. It speaks as if the shift has already occurred, because it understands that the mind bends around repeated certainty.

Instead of "I hope I can change," the language becomes: "I am changing." Instead of "Maybe I'll get through this," the imprint becomes: "This is already being handled." The difference is not just motivational. It is *functional*. The brain organizes itself around identity-driven speech. If you speak as if you are already becoming, you reinforce the becoming. If you speak as if you're still doubting, you reinforce the doubt.

This also applies to how you narrate your daily experiences. If something goes wrong and you tell yourself, "This always happens to me," that's not just a reaction — it's an imprint. You've just reinforced a self-image of helplessness. And your subconscious logs it. Not once. Every time.

Language becomes identity when it is repeated, emotionally charged, and unchallenged. The more often you speak a phrase that aligns with disempowerment — and the less you correct it — the deeper that phrase sinks in. Over time, your reality becomes a reflection of those unchecked scripts.

To break this cycle, you must develop language awareness. You must *audit* the phrases you repeat most often, especially when triggered. Not to judge yourself, but to identify where your own words are programming a reality you don't want.

The most effective reprogramming happens not through grand declarations, but through subtle, consistent rewrites of internal language. One of the most potent tools is the *daily imprint phrase*. This is a short, identity-anchored sentence that you repeat internally throughout the day, especially during micro-transitions — when you wake up, when you step into a new task, when you feel hesitation rising.

The key is emotional precision. A phrase like "I am powerful" only works if it lands with depth. If your system doesn't believe it yet, it will reject it. But if you shift it to something like "I am becoming someone who acts with power in every choice," your mind recognizes that as possible and starts reorganizing around it. Power phrases must sit on the edge of belief — believable enough to slip past resistance, strong enough to stretch your reality.

To make these phrases imprint, repetition isn't enough. You need *intensity*. Imprints form when thought, language, and emotional charge converge.

This is why moments of strong emotion — whether joy or pain — leave lasting psychological impressions. If you attach intention to those emotional surges, you can hijack that same mechanism for reprogramming.

So when you speak a power phrase, it's not a casual statement. You speak it with focus. With breath. With presence. You don't just say "I decide who I am." You *feel* the decision in your body when you say it. You look yourself in the mirror and say it through your posture, your tone, your silence after the words land. That is what imprints.

The same applies to the internal voice. Most people have a default monologue that has been running for decades. It was shaped by criticism, comparison, failure, social conditioning. But it can be interrupted. You don't need to silence it — you need to *override* it. When the old voice says, "You always mess this up," your job is not just to negate it but to replace it: "That's not me anymore. I execute with clarity now." That replacement must happen instantly and consistently, until the system accepts it as the new baseline.

Neuroscience supports this. The brain has what's known as "neuroplasticity," meaning it can reshape its pathways through repeated thought and behavior. But that plasticity is directionless — it follows repetition and emotion, not morality or truth. That's why painful phrases stick so easily. But once you understand this mechanism, you can use it with surgical precision. You speak the phrase. You inject the emotion. You do it over and over. The wiring rewrites itself. Not overnight, but inevitably.

If you want a faster pathway, tie language to movement. Physicalize the imprint. When you speak a new phrase, anchor it to a gesture — a hand movement, a breath, a shift in posture. This creates a somatic link that deepens the command. Over time, just doing the movement will re-activate the phrase, and vice versa. You're training your nervous system to associate that motion with the new identity.

One final piece. Mental imprinting is not just about affirmations. It's about the language you allow into your environment. Pay attention to the conversations you stay in. The media you consume. The tone of voice you tolerate. Every input is a micro-script. Every word you absorb is either reinforcing the self you're building or pulling you back toward the one you're shedding.

Protect your mental field as if it were sacred code. Because it is. If someone speaks to you in a way that reduces your power, interrupt the signal. If your environment echoes old patterns, change the soundtrack. You're not just rewiring your brain — you're curating the language of your reality.

This is what it means to become the author of your system. Not by wishing, but by speaking with conscious intent. Not by escaping the voice in your head, but by training it to echo the identity you are here to install. The language of power is not decoration. It is the very architecture of transformation. Speak it, live it, and your mind will follow.

Part II. The Core Override

There's a threshold you cross when you realize that the problem is no longer the world around you. It's not your circumstances. It's not even your thoughts. It's the architecture behind the thoughts. The deep, hidden framework that decides *which* thoughts show up, *how* you interpret the world, and *who* you unconsciously keep becoming.

Most people never reach this point. They stay locked in surface-level change — switching habits, repeating affirmations, trying to "think positively." But if you're here, it means you're done with patchwork fixes. You're ready to go deeper. You're ready to override the core.

This is where real transformation begins. Not in the conscious mind, but in the patterns beneath it — the layers where identity, belief, memory, and meaning were fused together long before you knew you had a choice. This part of the system doesn't respond to logic. It doesn't care about what you "should" believe or what you "want" to feel. It obeys only one thing: imprint.

This is the operating system that's been running your entire life in the background. It determines your perception of what's possible, what you're worth, how others respond to you, and even what kind of opportunities you're allowed to notice. And until you reprogram this level, every change you try to make will snap back to the original code.

Part II is about breaking that code at its source. Not by force, but by precision. You're going to learn how to reach the emotional and neurological root of the loops you've been living in. You'll dismantle the default settings that were never yours to begin with — the ones installed by family, media, culture, trauma, repetition. Then you'll begin the process of replacing them with systems you design, deliberately and consciously.

But let's be clear: this isn't mindset work. This is system override. This is the part where you take the mental mechanisms that have been shaping your life, and you begin to rebuild them from the inside out — using language, attention, sensation, and choice as tools of internal engineering.

You'll learn to detect the exact moment a limiting belief tries to assert itself — and override it before it becomes emotion, identity, or action. You'll intercept mental scripts that used to run automatically, and interrupt their power. Most importantly, you'll begin to install a dominant identity so clear and reinforced that it becomes your new baseline.

This isn't theoretical. It's visceral. You're not just changing thoughts — you're shifting your entire neural architecture. The Core Override isn't about becoming someone new. It's about remembering the version of you that was buried under scripts you didn't write — and giving that version the authority to take control.

This part of the process will demand your full presence. It will ask you to choose power over comfort, precision over noise, and truth over habit. But if you commit, what you'll find on the other side isn't just a better version of yourself.

It's the original one — finally unlocked.

Chapter 3: Seal the Subconscious Gateway

Sensory Seals: Guarding What Programs You

Every single day, your nervous system is absorbing more than your conscious mind can process. Sounds, images, sensations, colors, voices, symbols, tones, body language, and background noise all come in through the senses. And most of it doesn't get filtered. It gets stored.

You might think you're in control of your thoughts. But most of your thoughts are being fed by what you're exposed to — not what you consciously choose. What you hear, see, and feel repeatedly doesn't just pass through you. It **shapes** you. It becomes part of your inner code.

This is why the concept of *sensory seals* exists. A sensory seal is not about shutting the world out. It's about creating a filter strong enough to guard what enters your inner system. Because if your senses are open channels — and they are — then everything you allow in is a form of programming. The music in your background. The tone of someone's voice. The way a character is portrayed in a show. The subtle despair in a news anchor's face. The fake empowerment in an ad. None of it is neutral.

The truth is, most people have no seals at all. Their minds are constantly being hijacked by what they didn't even notice they let in. Their mood is altered by music that vibrates with emptiness. Their sense of worth is shaped by the pixels of a filtered body on their screen. Their perception of danger or safety is tilted by the pacing of a news clip. They are constantly being programmed without permission.

But once you see this, you can't unsee it. You realize your reality isn't entirely yours. It's been co-authored by external stimuli you never consented to. This isn't paranoia — this is precision. Because without a deliberate sensory seal, your internal world will always be vulnerable to invisible influence.

This is especially dangerous for someone who is *rewiring*. In the early stages of NPT, your system is more plastic, more open. You're actively changing old neural loops. That also means you're more impressionable. If you don't seal your senses with intention, the very wiring you're trying to overwrite may get reinforced again by external noise.

It's like trying to reprogram a computer while leaving it connected to a virus-infected network. No matter how clean the code you try to install, the corruption keeps slipping back in. To protect the code, you need a firewall. That's what sensory seals are.

A seal isn't something physical. It's an energetic and neurological boundary. You set it through awareness and repetition. You train your brain to question what it's exposed to before allowing it inside. You teach your system to treat your senses as sacred ports of entry. What enters must pass a filter.

You don't need to isolate yourself from the world. That's not power. What's powerful is to be in the world and still remain sovereign over your mind. That requires conscious filtration — a seal that protects without hardening, filters without fear, and allows in only what serves your highest programming.

Let's begin to understand how sensory data actually gets embedded. Once you see the mechanics, you'll know how to control the input.

Your brain doesn't distinguish between real and simulated input as much as you think it does. If a sound, image, or phrase carries enough emotional charge or repetition, your nervous system logs it as significant. It leaves an imprint. Advertisers have known this for decades. So have propaganda machines. The key isn't truth. The key is exposure and frequency.

Now ask yourself: what are you exposed to most? What's on your feed? What plays in your ears when you're not thinking? What are the dominant tones, moods, and messages running in the background of your daily life?

If you want to shift your internal code, you must curate your sensory environment with the same precision you'd use to protect your most sensitive data. You don't need to cut everything out. But you do need to take control of what gets inside and how often it gets repeated.

Start small. Remove input that feels subtly depleting. Silence noise that leaves you agitated or drained without knowing why. Replace chaotic stimulation with clarity. Music that centers you. Words that restore you. Visuals that carry signal, not noise. Your environment begins to reflect your intention.

It's not about always staying "positive." That's not strength. Strength is clarity. When your system is clear, you're no longer susceptible to every emotional cue embedded in someone else's message. You begin to choose your state instead of absorbing one.

This practice also reshapes your baseline. Many people live with overstimulated, scattered attention and think it's normal. Their inner state is not one they chose. It's one they were programmed into. Through constant dopamine spikes, erratic visuals, emotionally charged content, and overstimulation, the mind adapts to dysfunction as if it were baseline.

Once you seal your senses, the noise dies down. You begin to feel the subtleties of your own nervous system again. You hear your actual thoughts, not the ones triggered by suggestion. You notice how often your emotions are mimicked, not generated from within. You start to reclaim authorship.

This also restores your ability to focus. The mind that is not constantly hijacked by external signals becomes sharp. It becomes dangerous in the best way. It stops leaking energy. It starts to build power. And that power multiplies when you pair it with conscious input.

Your sensory seal isn't only about what you remove. It's about what you *install*. You can saturate your space with frequencies that elevate. You can embed your environment with anchors of power. A phrase on your wall that shifts your posture. A sound that centers you into your body. A symbol that reminds you who you are when you forget. These are not decorations. These are codes.

You can even design micro-imprints. A few seconds of intentional sound. A single word spoken daily with presence. A shift in lighting that signals clarity. These things add up. Your system responds to ritual. If your environment becomes aligned with the reality you are installing, your internal resistance dissolves faster. It no longer has to fight against the atmosphere. The atmosphere becomes your reinforcement.

You don't have to do this all at once. But once you begin, you'll notice the difference fast. The noise outside will feel louder — not because it got worse, but because your baseline got clearer. You'll sense the pull of old stimuli and realize how much they drained you. You'll start to feel the integrity of your system when it's no longer leaking from every open sensory gate.

This is the real reason most people can't shift. It's not that they're not doing the inner work. It's that their outer input keeps rewriting it. You cannot rewrite your neural code while exposing yourself to things that contradict it every day.

Seal it. Guard it. Then design it.

Because whatever you let in, programs you. And if you're not programming yourself, someone else is doing it for you.

Silent Influence: Words That Rewrite from Within

You don't always notice it, but language is running beneath the surface of your mind like a background process. It shapes your perception before you even speak. It determines how you interpret silence, how you process a look, how you predict the outcome of a conversation before it begins. And most of that happens without a single word being spoken aloud.

Language is not just communication. It's internal architecture. It wires associations, triggers emotional states, and organizes your sense of self in patterns so familiar they become invisible. The words you use privately — the way you speak to yourself in moments of decision, doubt, or discomfort — aren't just habits. They're scripts. And those scripts silently author your reality.

Think about it. You hesitate before acting because of a phrase like "what if I mess this up." You avoid confrontation because a sentence from the past still echoes: "don't make a scene." You downplay your power because of a buried command like "don't be too much." These aren't random thoughts. They're imprints. And they run deep.

The mistake most people make is believing that their internal dialogue is just a reflection of how they feel. In reality, it's the mechanism by which those feelings are reinforced and looped. The words generate the emotion. Then the emotion justifies the words. And the loop feeds itself.

This is how beliefs are embedded: not through one major decision, but through hundreds of small verbal choices repeated in quiet moments. Over time, they define your identity. Not because you consciously chose them, but because you didn't know you were being programmed.

That's where silent influence becomes powerful. Because once you understand how words shape your internal field, you can start to intercept them. You can insert language patterns that rewrite from within — phrases that act like internal upgrades, overriding the ones that no longer serve you. But it can't just be surface-level affirmation. You can't repeat things you don't believe and expect your subconscious to comply. The words must be rooted in precision. They must speak to the part of you that already knows. Not to convince it, but to awaken it.

For example, if the old loop says, "I never get it right," the upgrade isn't simply "I always succeed." That sounds false to the nervous system. The real upgrade might sound like, "I calibrate faster every time." It speaks to progress, not perfection. It aligns with the body's truth. And because of that, it lands. It sticks. It builds.

This is the art of internal language engineering. You speak to the system in a code it can accept, rather than trying to force it into submission with empty positivity. You choose words that resonate with your nervous system's current capacity while pointing it toward expansion.

This requires awareness. You must listen to the exact phrasing that governs your reactions. You must catch the moments you say things like "I always mess this up," "this always happens to me," or "I'm not built for this." Not just because they're disempowering, but because they're hypnotic. Every time you say them, even mentally, you deepen the neural path that supports them.

To reverse that, you don't need a full speech. You need one sentence. One sentence that carries the correct emotional tone, precision, and rhythm — and repeats often enough to install a new baseline.

This is where we begin the deeper work. What follows is not just about recognizing language. It's about learning how to encode it, layer it, and install it from the inside out.

Let's begin with the primary shift: the transition from unconscious phrasing to conscious imprinting.

Conscious imprinting begins with intentional phrasing, but it doesn't end there. The power of a phrase is not just in the words themselves, but in how they are delivered internally. The tone you use, the timing, the level of attention you bring to the moment you say it — these act as carriers for the message. They signal to the subconscious whether this information is important enough to integrate.

You've already seen this process used against you. Commercials don't just deliver words. They pair them with music, colors, movement, emotion. The message becomes immersive, and that's what makes it stick. The nervous system registers it not as a passing thought, but as an experience. When you reverse engineer this, you can use the same mechanics to your benefit.

To install a new phrase, you must slow it down. Strip it of clutter. Speak it internally with deliberate weight. If it's meant to replace an old reflex — like "I can't handle this"   then it needs to be spoken precisely at the moment the old pattern usually fires. That's when the nervous system is open. That's when the gate to rewiring is active.

You may find at first that the new phrase feels unfamiliar. That's normal. The brain is designed to favor the known over the new, even if the known is painful. Familiarity equals safety. But when a phrase is repeated often enough, and paired with even slight relief or clarity, the brain begins to prefer it. It starts to anchor it in memory. Over time, this new language becomes your new lens.

The difference is subtle but powerful. Instead of thinking "I'm overwhelmed," your system starts to hear "I'm stabilizing." Instead of "I'm not ready," it starts to hear "I'm adjusting to capacity." These shifts don't just change mood. They change trajectory. They move you out of survival loops and into forward movement, quietly and consistently.

There's a deeper layer to this. When you begin to use language that upgrades your state, you also change how people experience you. Others pick up on the internal phrases you carry. Not because they hear them, but because your tone, posture, and presence are shaped by them. Influence begins in the body, and language is one of its strongest sculptors.

That's why those who carry silent influence don't always speak often. They don't need to. Their internal language is already shaping the field. They walk into a room with an invisible clarity. Their decisions feel final without being forceful. Their silence carries weight because their inner world is not full of noise. It is full of command.

To reach this level, your language must become clean. No internal sarcasm, no habitual self-dismissal, no muttered negativity disguised as realism. Each time you engage in those, you distort your frequency. You scatter your influence. And you weaken the imprint you're trying to build.

The discipline is in the repetition. It's in the way you speak to yourself while walking alone, while getting dressed, while preparing for a difficult conversation. You are not just thinking. You are setting codes. And those codes will determine what your nervous system expects, how it reacts, and what it seeks out in your environment.

You don't need to become hypervigilant or robotic. You need to become deliberate. Choose phrases that ground you in clarity, not fantasy. Use words that reconnect you to center, not inflate an illusion. Speak as if your mind listens to everything you say — because it does.

The influence you carry begins inside. It isn't earned through external effort alone. It's installed through quiet, consistent self-command. And the most powerful reprogramming often happens in the sentences no one hears but you.

How to Install a Trigger Phrase to Block Old Conditioning

Every conditioned pattern in the brain begins with a cue. Something you see, feel, think, or anticipate activates the same loop you've played for years. These loops aren't just mental. They are deeply physical. Your body responds as if it already knows what's about to happen, and it plays out the reaction with precision. But precision does not mean intelligence. Most of your conditioned responses were built in moments of stress, fear, or repetition — not conscious choice.

This is where the trigger phrase becomes your edge. Instead of allowing the cue to spiral into the old reflex, you intercept it with a phrase that redirects the nervous system. The right phrase, installed correctly, can halt the momentum of an unconscious reaction before it overtakes you.

To be effective, the phrase must meet several conditions. First, it must feel authoritative. Not in a way that mimics punishment or force, but in a way that feels centered and certain. A shaky phrase — something tentative or abstract — won't break the rhythm of a strong conditioned loop. Second, it must be simple enough to remember and strong enough to cut through emotional noise. And third, it must be repeated in the exact moments that matter, when the loop is about to begin.

Let's say your old pattern is spiraling into self-doubt during moments of challenge. It might begin with a thought like "I don't know if I can handle this," followed by a physical contraction, mental distraction, and the urge to withdraw or delay. You've run this loop countless times, so your system recognizes it and executes it quickly.

Now imagine you insert a phrase like "Pattern recognized. I choose differently." The moment that first thought surfaces, the phrase is activated. You speak it internally — slowly, clearly, as if issuing a command to your system. That phrase becomes the new cue. It disrupts the script before it unfolds.

But here's what matters most: the trigger phrase is not just a sentence. It must be paired with a micro-shift in your physical state. A straightening of your spine. A breath drawn deeper than usual. A moment of silence where you wait before reacting. This pairing is what tells the nervous system that something different is happening.

If you only say the phrase but remain in the same collapsed posture or shallow breathing, your body won't believe you. It will override the phrase and default to the old program. The mind follows the body. A subtle but deliberate state change is required to make the phrase land.

This is not about pretending. It's about creating a micro-interruption in the default loop. That interruption gives you just enough space to make a new choice. And that space — even if it's just three seconds long — is where the reprogramming happens.

You don't need to make the phrase sound motivational. In fact, it shouldn't sound like hype. It should feel like a calm authority taking the wheel. Something like "Not this path" or "I'm here. I'm choosing." Even "Pause. Observe. Reset." The exact wording is yours to decide, but the structure should feel like a signal — not a plea.

What you're installing is not just a tool. It's a neural gatekeeper. Once installed, this phrase becomes part of your mental infrastructure. Its power comes from consistency. The more often you use it, especially in the heat of the trigger moment, the more quickly it becomes automatic. Eventually, the loop doesn't run at all. The phrase fires first.

Now that the foundations are laid, we can go deeper into the specific steps of installation and reinforcement. That's where the shift becomes long-term.

To hardwire the phrase into your nervous system, it must be tested under real conditions. Mental rehearsal is the preparation. Real-life activation is the reinforcement. Every time you notice the familiar tension beginning to rise — in thought, breath, or posture — you fire the phrase. Don't wait until the full emotional cascade is underway. The power is in catching the first flicker.

At the beginning, you might only notice the old loop after it's halfway through. That's not failure. That's awareness forming. You use that moment anyway. Even mid-pattern, speak the phrase. Breathe. Reset your posture. Doing so interrupts the loop in progress and tells your system, "Even now, it's not too late to change course."

Repetition in calm moments also builds strength. When your body is relaxed and your mind is still, repeating the phrase plants it deeper. The nervous system is more receptive when it's not in survival mode. Ten repetitions in a quiet state have more impact than fifty repetitions when you're already triggered.

47

Tie the phrase to breath. Each inhale is an opportunity to install, each exhale an opportunity to release the old. Say the phrase mentally on the inhale, let go of resistance on the exhale. This breath-linking technique turns the phrase into a rhythm, not just a thought. Over time, the breath itself can become the activator. A single intentional breath calls up the phrase, which stops the loop.

If you notice resistance or doubt when using the phrase — a part of you saying, "This isn't working," or "This feels fake" — acknowledge it. That voice is part of the old identity protecting its territory. You don't fight it. You include it in the awareness. "Even this resistance is part of the pattern." Then you return to the phrase.

Eventually, the phrase becomes reflexive. You'll notice the loop try to start, and before it can finish its first step, the phrase interrupts it. Not through willpower, but because the nervous system has learned a new sequence. The loop runs into a locked door. A door you built.

You may decide to create different trigger phrases for different categories of patterns. One for fear spirals, one for self-sabotage, one for people-pleasing. That level of precision can help in advanced stages, but in the beginning, one master phrase is enough. Simplicity wins when you're rewiring.

This phrase is not meant to erase your emotions. You are not shutting down your experience. You are interrupting the automatic, conditioned interpretation of that experience. Instead of feeling discomfort and instantly turning it into self-blame or avoidance, the phrase steps in and says, "This is sensation, not identity. Stay."

With consistent use, the phrase starts to create space. And in that space, you begin to see the mechanics of your mind. The speed slows down. The story weakens. You no longer assume the old meaning is true just because it's loud. You start to notice choice where there used to be only reaction.

Eventually, your relationship to thought itself shifts. You stop assuming that every narrative running through your mind deserves obedience. The phrase is the wedge. It creates just enough separation between the inner voice and the one hearing it.

That's where freedom begins — not in controlling every thought, but in breaking the illusion that you have no choice. The trigger phrase is a subtle but powerful tool to wake you up at the precise point where you used to fall asleep. It doesn't need to shout. It just needs to be there, every time it counts.

Chapter 4: Interrupt the Default Pattern

The Subconscious Loves Predictable Loops

The subconscious mind isn't creative in the way most people imagine. It doesn't improvise, question, or evaluate. It repeats. Not because it's limited, but because repetition is what it trusts. Safety, to the subconscious, lies in what has been done before — regardless of whether it's actually helpful or harmful.

If you wake up every morning, check your phone, feel slightly overwhelmed, breathe shallowly, and tell yourself you're already behind, that sequence becomes a loop. Not just a mental habit, but a neural groove. Do it enough times and the body will trigger it automatically. Your biology begins to expect it. And because it's predictable, it becomes preferred.

The subconscious favors these loops for one reason: efficiency. It doesn't waste energy thinking about new responses when old ones are already mapped. The emotional reaction you had to a stressful email two years ago is the same one your system may summon again today — not because it's the best choice, but because it's already installed.

This explains why even painful patterns feel oddly familiar. Why someone can feel more comfortable in anxiety than in peace. Or why people sabotage things going well. On a conscious level, they want ease and expansion. But the subconscious clings to familiarity. It resists the unknown, even if the unknown holds relief.

The subconscious doesn't operate based on logic. It operates based on known rhythms. It's like a musician who only plays the songs it already knows by heart. Any deviation, no matter how slight, triggers internal alarms. You can try to override it consciously, but if you don't install a new rhythm underneath, the old track will keep playing.

This is why information alone doesn't create transformation. You can read books, take courses, hear inspiring insights, but if your daily rhythm still reflects the same loops — the same emotional beats, the same thoughts at the same times — then your subconscious assumes nothing has changed. It keeps firing the same sequence.

What most people call "feeling stuck" is this exact mechanism. Not a lack of intelligence or motivation, but a nervous system caught in a loop it has learned to associate with survival. The loop may include overthinking, procrastination, people-pleasing, numbing, or catastrophizing. And it happens not because it makes sense, but because it's familiar.

It's not just thoughts that loop. Emotions, postures, reactions, tone of voice — all can become part of a looped pattern. A slight tension in the shoulders may coincide with a particular internal dialogue. That posture becomes part of the loop. You feel the tension, the thought fires, the breath shallows, the loop completes.

To the subconscious, every part of the loop reinforces the others. Break one link, and the whole sequence begins to lose power. But without conscious disruption, it will repeat endlessly. You don't need to destroy the subconscious. You need to train it differently.

One of the most powerful ways to do this is through **pattern interruption paired with repetition**. Not a random change here or there, but a deliberate reprogramming where the new rhythm is practiced consistently. Only then does the subconscious start to see the new pattern as safe. It needs to *feel* the new rhythm enough times to start predicting it.

The key lies in frequency and intentionality. You are not trying to make a one-time change that the subconscious will accept immediately. You are gradually shifting what it recognizes as home. This means choosing new emotional setpoints, internal dialogues, and micro-behaviors that replace the old cues with new ones.

A person who has lived most of their life inside a loop of anxious hyper-vigilance will not instantly feel safe in calm. At first, calm will feel suspicious. Silence will feel wrong. Ease will feel empty. That is not a flaw. That is the subconscious flagging the unfamiliar as unsafe. But if calm becomes a repeated experience — even for one minute at a time — the subconscious begins adjusting its baseline. The old loop weakens. The new one grows.

This is also why self-sabotage is often misunderstood. The mind is not broken. It is simply operating under a set of instructions that were never questioned. What feels like failure is often just the pull of the old groove, trying to reclaim its dominance. You don't erase that groove by fighting it. You override it by consistently choosing something else, again and again, until the new groove becomes stronger.

The mistake many people make is expecting the change to feel immediately empowering. Often, it doesn't. It feels awkward, uncertain, or even fake. That discomfort is the sign that you are no longer in the old loop. But unless you recognize that discomfort as progress, the tendency will be to go back to what feels familiar, even if that familiar rhythm keeps you small.

To truly break the loop, you must become deliberate about your sensory and emotional inputs. What you hear, say, feel, and see every day creates neural tone. If the majority of what surrounds you supports the old loop — noise, stress, criticism, fatigue — then that's what your system will keep responding to. Shifting the inputs is not about denial. It's about creating a field where the new pattern can take root.

A person who wants to move from self-doubt to confidence must build a loop that contains confident action. Even small ones. Speaking clearly in situations where they used to shrink. Making a decision without apologizing for it. Changing posture. Repeating phrases internally that reflect the identity they are stepping into. The subconscious cannot reject consistency. It is wired to follow what is rehearsed.

None of this is about perfection. Missing a day does not break the process. It's about returning to the rhythm and reinforcing it. The subconscious, unlike the conscious mind, does not care about complexity. It responds to emotional energy and repetition. If something evokes a clear emotional tone and is repeated often enough, it will begin to install itself automatically.

Eventually, the old loop begins to decay. It stops firing with the same intensity. You'll notice the thoughts still arise, but they lack weight. The reactions still whisper, but they don't grab. That's a sign that the loop is losing its grip. It is being overwritten by something more coherent with who you are choosing to become.

You do not have to escape your subconscious. You need to teach it what to trust. And trust, for the subconscious, is built through what is practiced. When your internal environment reflects the same tone over and over, your subconscious will lock onto it. Not because it was convinced, but because it was shown.

This is how the deeper shift happens. Not by fighting the loop, but by becoming the one who authors it. The moment your rhythm becomes more intentional than automatic, the entire system begins to reorganize. That is the doorway to reprogramming. That is how the loop breaks.

Reverse the Pattern, Break the Circuit

Some patterns don't need to be healed. They need to be reversed.

When you're caught in a behavioral or emotional loop, the problem isn't always the content of the thoughts. It's the automatic nature of the reaction. The brain is firing along a well-worn path, and your nervous system is locked into a role: respond, comply, collapse, avoid, overcompensate. This loop becomes so predictable that it begins to override your actual perception of what's happening in the moment. You're not responding to reality — you're responding to the past, rehearsed as the present.

To break the loop, you have to do what the loop doesn't expect.

If you always freeze when confronted, speak. If you always argue when threatened, stay quiet. If your default is to people-please, say no. This isn't about performing the opposite for the sake of it. It's about disrupting the circuit by refusing to follow the script it's trying to run. The mind expects the usual signal. You interrupt it with a new one.

This principle is simple but not easy. The old pattern has emotional weight. It might come with anxiety, urgency, or a sense of internal pressure. That's the current running through the circuit, trying to push you back into familiar territory. The task isn't to erase that feeling, but to override it with a new action — one that breaks the circuit in real time.

Imagine this like flipping a magnetic polarity. You're not trying to push harder against the pull. You're inverting the charge. And that shift scrambles the signal just enough to weaken its automatic pull. The loop can't run if the sequence is interrupted.

But here's the trap: the pattern will often disguise itself as logic. It will sound reasonable, even protective. "Just keep quiet." "Now isn't the time." "You're overreacting." It offers these lines not because they're true, but because they've worked before. They've kept the loop alive.

To reverse the pattern, you have to stop asking if it feels natural and start asking if it's new. Discomfort in this process is not a warning sign. It's often a signal that you are stepping out of the circuitry that has defined your identity. That tension is the exact space where the old wiring loses control.

Let's say you have a pattern of staying silent when something violates your boundaries. You think you're keeping the peace, but what you're really doing is reinforcing a loop of suppression and resentment. To break it, you don't need a long conversation or perfect timing. You need a single

53

sentence: "That's not okay with me." The words might shake. Your body might resist. But that sentence is a reversal. And that reversal breaks the loop.

Or maybe your pattern is to escape whenever something feels overwhelming. You run, emotionally or physically, and convince yourself that avoidance is survival. But the real break happens when you stay. Not frozen. Not waiting. Present. Grounded. That single moment of staying when your nervous system is screaming to run is the reversal. That is the beginning of rewiring.

This is not about becoming a different person. It's about reclaiming authorship over what gets to run your system. When you reverse the pattern once, it becomes easier to do it again. You start to see that the loop was never permanent — it just needed enough repetition to survive.

The repetition of reversal is what builds the new identity. But it must be felt, not just conceptualized.

The shift begins when you no longer wait to feel ready. Readiness is a trap the loop designed to keep you rehearsing instead of rewiring. Every time you act without full certainty, you weaken the loop's hold. You create instability in the circuit. And that instability is exactly what you want.

Your mind will often seek safety in explanation. It wants to understand why you react the way you do before allowing change. But this creates a stall. You don't need full psychological clarity to break a pattern. You need a moment of disobedience. A crack in the usual behavior. The analysis can come later, and it will be deeper because it's no longer filtered through the lens of the old identity.

Let your body be the lead indicator. When you notice tightness, contraction, shallow breath — that's your signal. These aren't signs to retreat. They're signs that a loop is active and can now be disrupted. Don't try to feel better. Do differently. That's the entire axis of transformation here.

This doesn't mean you push through every fear or override all internal resistance. The aim is precision, not aggression. Choose one point where the pattern usually wins, and flip it. One moment where you would normally comply, and you don't. That reversal, if repeated, begins to send a new signal into the nervous system: this is no longer who we are.

What begins as an act of rebellion becomes a new rhythm. You might still hear the old command. You might still feel the old emotion. That's fine.

You're not trying to eliminate the program all at once. You're teaching it that you don't obey it anymore.

This is how your subconscious updates its maps. Not through thought, but through action. Every reversed response tells the brain: this is the new sequence. This is the new normal. And over time, the old pattern atrophies. It doesn't get the fuel it needs to keep running.

The breakthrough comes when you no longer see reversal as effort but as return. Return to choice, to authorship, to real-time agency. You no longer need to perform who you were. You are now forming who you become.

There's no perfection in this process. You will slip. You'll catch yourself repeating the old move. But the moment you notice, the pattern is already weakened. Awareness is the first reversal. You're not unconscious inside the circuit anymore. That single second of clarity is enough to tilt the whole thing off balance.

And when you do reverse the pattern, you'll feel it. The moment will feel unfamiliar, sometimes even awkward. But under that awkwardness is freedom. Not the kind of freedom you conceptualize, but the kind that reintroduces you to your own power. The kind that doesn't ask permission. Eventually, the pattern stops expecting you. It loses your participation. And that's the death of any loop: your refusal to repeat it.

You don't escape your programming by thinking about your past. You escape it by becoming unrecognizable to it in the present. And every moment you choose to reverse, you become more fluent in the language of who you're becoming.

This is how you stop being a reflection of your conditioning and start becoming the architect of your mind. Not with grand gestures, but with small, deliberate inversions of what no longer fits.

The system is not as fixed as it feels. It's just practiced. And whatever has been practiced can be unlearned.

Flip the signal. Break the sequence. Then do it again.

Rituals of Disruption: Creating Friction for Control

You are programmed to seek ease. The brain is wired to conserve energy, to move along paths of least resistance. This evolutionary trait is useful when you're navigating survival, but it becomes a liability when you're trying to reprogram your subconscious. Because ease does not build sovereignty. Friction does.

The friction we're speaking about here isn't struggle for the sake of pain. It's engineered tension. Conscious interference. You apply pressure to the system not to break it, but to reveal where it's running on default. Without friction, there's no disruption. And without disruption, there's no reprogramming.

This is where ritual enters.

Rituals of disruption are not mystical habits you perform at sunrise. They're deliberate insertions into your day that cause interruption. They make your comfort zones uncomfortable and your automatic patterns visible. These are not about optimization. They are about destabilization, on purpose.

Because when the system is disrupted, control becomes possible again. You wake up from automation. And in that space between stimulus and response, you gain leverage.

Most people live without this space. Their routines, reactions, and thoughts loop in predictable circuits. Even the rituals they do have—like morning routines or self-care checklists—often reinforce the same identity they're trying to transcend. That's why disruption must be intentional and intelligent. It's not about removing structure. It's about redesigning it.

A well-designed disruption doesn't need to be dramatic. It needs to be precise. Think of it like inserting a wedge into a gear. You don't need to stop the whole machine. You just need to interrupt one tooth of the wheel, and the entire motion hesitates. That hesitation is gold. That's where the rewrite begins.

Let's say your loop is reactivity—snapping when you feel disrespected. A ritual of disruption might be to say nothing at all for sixty seconds. Not out of repression, but awareness. That delay creates internal friction. It allows space for a new script to emerge. The delay is the ritual. The space is the control.

The point is not to replace reaction with suppression. The point is to practice an entirely different rhythm. A person operating from power doesn't obey their first impulse. They choose the one that holds weight, not noise.

Another example. If your mornings typically begin with digital consumption—checking messages, scrolling feeds, reacting to external inputs—then a disruption might be to remain in silence for the first ten minutes. Just ten. Long enough to feel the itch to react, and long enough to override it. That moment of tension is what you're after. That's when you're retraining your brain to obey you, not your addiction to stimulation.

You're not just changing habits. You're training perception. When rituals create friction, they also create sensitivity. You begin to notice what used to be invisible. The micro-compulsions. The auto-responses. The stories that were running your nervous system without your consent.

And it's not about volume. One strong ritual, repeated, is more effective than fifty scattered ones. The key is that it interrupts. Not for drama. Not for novelty. But for control.

The most effective rituals are not always visible to others. They are internal rewrites. You create a break in the flow of unconscious action and insert intention where none existed. This is where transformation occurs—not in loud declarations or public behaviors, but in the moments no one sees, where you choose awareness over reaction.

To create meaningful friction, start with where your patterns feel most automatic. It could be the way you scroll to escape discomfort, the tone you use when defending yourself, or the posture your body holds when you feel powerless. These are entry points. Small, but loaded with data.

The ritual is to notice, then disrupt. Not in a way that causes guilt or shame, but in a way that asserts your presence. This noticing is not passive. It's active, targeted observation. You're scanning for repetition. You're hunting the loop. And the moment you catch it in motion, you pause. That pause is not a void. It is a tool.

Most people avoid friction because it feels like failure. But friction is not resistance to be overcome. It is a message. It tells you the system is engaged, that the programming is running. Which means the moment is alive. This is where you can work.

This is why disruptive rituals must become part of your daily rhythm, not separate from it. They are not extras or add-ons. They are anchors. If done correctly, they evolve into your new autopilot. The initial disruption becomes the new code.

A well-placed ritual can also neutralize triggers before they gain momentum. For example, before entering a space where you tend to lose presence—like a meeting, a conversation with family, or a high-pressure task—you might create a micro-ritual: a breath pattern, a hand gesture, a short command whispered internally. It's not the action that holds the power, but the awareness it forces. It cues the nervous system: you are in control now.

Eventually, the act of disrupting becomes instinct. Not because you've forced it, but because you've layered it through repetition. Repetition carves neurological grooves. But only when done with presence. There is no magic in doing something daily unless the daily act carries conscious weight.

And here's the nuance: friction without structure becomes agitation. If you only disrupt but don't reorient, you stay stuck in resistance. That's why each disruptive ritual must have a direction. What are you interrupting? Why? And what do you want to install in its place?

Without these answers, you'll create chaos instead of change.

You don't need dozens of rituals. One or two that matter are enough. But they must be precise. Not grand, but sharp. They should touch the core of the loop you're rewriting. And they should not be pleasant. They should be powerful.

Disruption works because it activates attention. You cannot sleepwalk through a moment of friction. It forces your presence to come online. And presence is the one state the old code cannot survive in.

Eventually, these rituals rewire your emotional thresholds. What once triggered avoidance or collapse now becomes neutral. You reclaim access to your faculties. You override the circuitry that once owned you. That is power—not loud, not performative, but absolute.

What you're building isn't just discipline. It's authorship. You're becoming the one who decides what scripts run, what responses fire, what identity gets expressed. You stop being the sum of your programming. You start being the one who rewrites it, one precise disruption at a time.

Chapter 5: Command the Decision Layer

Micro-Decisions = Macro-Reality

Most people believe their life changes in big moments. A career leap, a breakup, a win, a loss. But those are just the visible markers. What actually shaped your reality were the micro-decisions you made long before and long after those events. The decision to check your phone instead of finish your project. The decision to walk away from the conversation instead of saying what mattered. The decision to stay silent when your intuition told you to speak.

These moments are small enough to ignore, which is exactly why they carry so much power. They pass beneath awareness. And because they seem insignificant, the mind doesn't fight them. You don't call them choices. You call them habits, personality, or just "how things are." But every time you choose a familiar reaction over a conscious response, you cast a vote for the identity you say you're trying to outgrow.

The subconscious doesn't care about your long-term goals. It only cares about consistency. And consistency is built on repetition. Not repetition of thought, but repetition of action. Micro-decisions are the material your subconscious uses to define what is safe, familiar, and true. This is how your internal system decides who you are.

Your brain wants certainty. So when you make the same small decision day after day, your system locks it in. It becomes your behavioral baseline. And from that baseline, your reality is filtered. What you notice. What you dismiss. What you tolerate. What you expect. All of it gets shaped by the quiet choices you keep making in the background.

This is why trying to "change your life" without changing your micro-decisions never works. You might get bursts of motivation or clarity, but if the small actions remain the same, the system pulls you back to the old script. Not because you're broken. Because your neural networks are efficient. The brain loves patterns it doesn't have to think about. It protects them, even when they hurt you.

So how do you shift this?

Not by pushing harder. Not by thinking more positively. But by identifying the handful of micro-moments that shape the direction of your day. The moments where you usually go into default. Where you check out. Numb. React. Comply. Escape. These are the leverage points.

They are often boring and easy to miss. They look like whether or not you get out of bed when the alarm rings. Whether or not you respond with patience when you feel criticized. Whether or not you choose the food that matches your energetic goals instead of your craving. These are not moral issues. They are control points.

What you consistently choose in those moments is what creates your future. Not the vision board or the big intention-setting ritual. Those things matter, but they are hollow without behavioral proof. And the proof is always found in the smallest acts.

You do not need to overhaul your entire life in one sweep. That's usually the quickest way to fail. What you need is precision. Start by choosing one area of life where you feel stuck, then trace it backward. Find the smallest fork in the road that keeps sending you down the same path. That fork is a micro-decision.

That story is the script. And every time you act it out without challenging it, you strengthen its hold on your subconscious. This is how reality gets reinforced. Not by intention alone, but by the accumulation of choices that align with a narrative you may not even believe in anymore.

Changing your script starts by creating friction. The brain won't naturally interrupt a pattern unless something disrupts its rhythm. You need to pause the loop just long enough to observe it instead of becoming it. This can be as simple as a breath, a deliberate question, or a physical gesture that grounds you back in the moment. The goal is not to win every micro-decision, but to make just one conscious enough that it begins to ripple.

One choice made with clarity can recalibrate your sense of identity. Not because it proves you're disciplined, but because it breaks the illusion that your actions are fixed. It reminds you that you are not the automation. You are the one who chooses what the system runs.

There is nothing mystical about this. You don't need to wait until you feel ready. The shift happens in the moment you recognize that a familiar impulse is trying to take the wheel, and you do something different. Not huge. Just different. That difference sends a signal to your subconscious. It tells your nervous system: we are no longer running the old program.

This is where a new reality begins.

A person who chooses to drink water instead of reach for sugar is not just being "healthy." They are communicating to their subconscious that short-term craving no longer runs the show. A person who pauses before sending a reactive message isn't just being calm. They are reassigning power away from emotion and toward vision. These moments are quiet. No one claps for them. But over time, they build a new architecture of self.

If you want to live in a different world, you must first prove to your nervous system that it's safe to be a different version of you. The micro-decisions are your way of doing that without force or overwhelm. They are the bridge between who you've been and who you are becoming.

Tracking these decisions gives you leverage. You start to notice that the loop you thought was fate is actually a habit. That what seemed inevitable was simply unexamined. As this awareness grows, the decisions you make stop being reactions. They become strategies.

And when that happens, the external world can't help but shift in response. Because the micro-patterns of action are the raw code that builds your day. Your day becomes your week. Your week becomes your month. And your months, over time, become your identity.

You don't need to fight for transformation. You just need to commit to a higher standard in the smallest, most ignored places. This is not about perfection. It's about loyalty to what you say matters. Even when no one is watching. Especially then.

Each micro-decision is either casting a vote for your past or your future. One is built on survival. The other on choice. You already know which one you're meant to follow. Now you prove it, in the quiet.

Installing Conscious Overrides in Trigger Moments

There's a specific moment, often just a fraction of a second, when everything inside you tightens. Your breathing shifts, your body stiffens, your thoughts accelerate or freeze. It's the moment before the reaction. The trigger.

Most people don't see that moment. They live inside it, owned by it. Their nervous system detects something familiar — a raised tone, a dismissive glance, a perceived rejection — and immediately defaults to the program it has run a thousand times. Anger. Withdrawal. Pleasing. Defensiveness. Whatever was wired in through repetition or trauma now acts on their behalf.

This is where the override must be installed.

You cannot eliminate all your triggers. Nor should you try. Triggers are access points. They reveal the blueprint of your conditioning. They show you exactly where the override is needed most. But to install it, you must first locate the space between trigger and action. You must learn to recognize the flicker of sensation before it becomes behavior.

This is the real work of reprogramming. Not just journaling about wounds, but meeting your system where it fires — in real time. When you feel the emotional hijack begin, your task is to disrupt the default. Not by suppressing it, but by consciously interrupting the sequence it usually follows.

This starts with pattern mapping.

Take a trigger that repeatedly pulls you out of alignment. Maybe it's someone questioning your intelligence. Maybe it's being ignored. Whatever it is, don't analyze it in the abstract. Track the actual steps it takes in your body. What tightens first? What does your inner voice say? What thoughts rush in? What is the first urge?

Then pause. Not after the behavior, but at the very first physical signal that something is about to take over. This is the entry point. This is where your override belongs.

The override itself must be simple, visceral, and practiced in advance. It is not a complex mantra or a concept to think about. It's a signal — a new pathway you embed in your system that, when activated, redirects your energy away from reaction and toward conscious authority.

Some people anchor this override in breath. A slow, sharp inhale through the nose, a hold, then a release. Not just to calm down, but to insert a deliberate act where previously there was only impulse. Others use a phrase, one that has been emotionally rehearsed to carry weight. Not something borrowed from a book, but a line that disrupts the story they usually fall into.

The phrase must speak directly to the part of you that gets hijacked. If your pattern is collapsing into shame, the phrase must restore power. If your pattern is rage, the phrase must center. This phrase is not said for others to hear. It is a private code, an internal redirect, designed to cut through the noise in the split-second when the pattern begins.

To make this override work, you must rehearse it outside of the trigger. You can't wait until you're overwhelmed. The brain won't reach for what's unfamiliar in a state of threat. It will default. So you create the override through repetition before you need it. You embed it not by force, but by choice. Every day. Until it becomes the new edge of who you are becoming. Every time you practice this override outside the trigger, you're teaching your nervous system that another option exists. You are not removing the emotion. You are building space around it. You are separating identity from impulse. That gap is not just psychological. It is physiological. You are changing the way your brain wires its responses by interrupting the auto-sequence and inserting conscious command.

This is not about control in the rigid sense. It's about authorship. The moment you insert the override, you re-enter the position of choice. You stop being a replay and become a decision. That decision, practiced once, is weak. Practiced daily, it becomes a governing structure. Your nervous system learns it the same way it learned the old response: through consistency, clarity, and emotional charge.

The override should be emotionally weighted. If your phrase feels flat, it won't hold in real moments. It has to land like a shift in posture, like a key turning in a lock. This is why it has to be personal. It must speak to the part of you that forgot it had power. It must summon the energy of the future self — the one who is already free from that loop.

When the override becomes familiar, your nervous system begins to reach for it naturally. What once took effort begins to feel like alignment. You will notice the trigger still exists, but its control weakens. The same words, the same glance, the same tone no longer pull you under. This is not repression. It is re-encoding.

There is a precision to when this override matters most. It's in the moments when you're most tempted to collapse into the old version. When someone disrespects you. When doubt hits. When loneliness spikes. Those are not just emotional moments. They are doorways. If you override at that point, even once, you reroute the loop. Not forever in that instant, but enough to start.

If you fail to install it perfectly at first, that's expected. Reconditioning doesn't begin with mastery. It begins with recognition. Even noticing that you missed the moment is progress. It proves you are no longer merged with the trigger. You've begun to observe it. That awareness is the foothold. With each attempt, the override grows stronger. It becomes less about discipline and more about identity. This is who I am now. Not because you forced it, but because you repeated it until it replaced the old imprint.

Eventually, what used to be your override becomes your baseline. You won't need to pause as often because you'll find yourself responding as the new self automatically. The system that once betrayed you with reflexes will begin to reflect the code you consciously wrote. That is when you know the installation has taken root.

And still, even then, you remain a student of the trigger. Life will evolve to present more refined patterns, more subtle versions of old wounds. But with each one, your override strengthens. It doesn't make you numb. It makes you clear. You are not deleting emotion. You are reclaiming the authority to respond with intention. That is the edge. That is the mark of a reprogrammed mind.

There is no final moment of being trigger-proof. There is only greater speed, deeper awareness, and increasing command. The override is not just a tool. It's a threshold. Each time you activate it, you are stepping across the old identity and walking as the one who codes their own reality. Not in theory, not in private, but in the most reactive, vulnerable spaces — where power is either reclaimed or lost.

And in choosing the override, you are choosing who gets to speak for you. You are choosing your future in real time.

The Mental Pause That Rewires Everything

There is a split second between stimulus and response that most people never notice. It's small, quiet, and easy to miss. But that space is where transformation happens. It's the space where you can insert something new. Not just a better behavior, but a deeper interruption. One that rewrites the script your nervous system has been following unconsciously for years.

Most of your life has been shaped by what you do in automatic mode. You feel discomfort, and your system reacts. You hear criticism, and your system responds. These patterns play out faster than thought. They're embedded not just in the mind, but in the body. Muscle tension, tone of voice, facial expression — all of it part of a familiar, conditioned sequence. This is the architecture of reflexive living. And until you disrupt it, it will keep running your reality.

The mental pause is not simply about "taking a breath." It's about learning to *catch* the moment before the program takes over. That moment contains choice. That choice, when practiced, becomes power. But power only exists when awareness is present. Without awareness, you're just reliving memory in motion — your past reacting to your present.

Think about how quickly you justify a reaction. The story comes in immediately. "They disrespected me." "I always mess this up." "This is just how I am." But these aren't truths. They're just rehearsed closures. The mental pause is your refusal to collapse into that closure. It doesn't ask you to suppress. It asks you to hold. And in that holding, you create a new condition for the mind: stillness without submission.

This stillness doesn't mean numbness. It's a state of awake neutrality. It's when you observe what your system wants to do, and choose to do nothing — just yet. That gap rewires more than you can see. It creates a rupture in the loop. And that rupture, if reinforced, becomes a new circuit.

When you pause, you are not avoiding action. You are elevating the level of consciousness from which you act. You're stepping out of reactive programming and into authored response. This is not passive. It's precision. Because what you do from the pause holds more impact than anything done from default.

The nervous system doesn't like this at first. It sees the pause as unfamiliar, and unfamiliar equals unsafe. You may feel an urge to speak, lash out, pull away, explain, escape. But if you can stay — even just for a few breaths —

you interrupt the cascade. Your heart rate may slow. Your body may tremble. Your mind may argue. Let it. These are signs the old loop is losing its grip.

Over time, that pause becomes something your system recognizes. It learns that it's not a threat, but a threshold. The more you cross it, the easier it becomes to stay centered in chaos. You begin to notice the moment as it arises — not after the damage is done, but while it's still moldable. You gain access to the invisible hinge that turns reaction into response.

The key is not just in practicing this once or twice, but in embedding it into your daily awareness. It doesn't require rituals or silence or solitude. It just requires intention. Intention to catch the edge of reactivity before it owns you. And that edge is always closer than you think.

The real strength of the pause is that it teaches the system to respond from clarity rather than compulsion. This doesn't mean becoming emotionless or detached. On the contrary, the pause gives you fuller access to the truth beneath the emotional flare. It lets you hear the real need beneath the reaction. The need might be to feel safe, seen, respected, or simply to be understood. When you pause, you give space for the need to emerge before the story hijacks it.

This shift is not conceptual. It must be embodied. The body is where the loop begins, and it's also where it ends. So the pause isn't just a thought — it's a physical choice. When you feel heat rising, jaw clenching, hands tightening, or shoulders bracing, that's the gateway. Instead of moving forward with the familiar pattern, you stay right there. You don't try to fix it or change it. You simply notice, stay, and breathe with precision. Not to calm yourself, but to anchor attention into the present.

That's the difference. Most people breathe to escape. But this kind of breath is a form of entry. A way to bring consciousness into the body without pushing anything away. Over time, this trains the nervous system to expand its window of tolerance. What once triggered panic or defense now becomes tolerable. And eventually, what becomes tolerable becomes transformable.

It's important to understand that the mind will fight this. Especially if it has always used speed as a coping mechanism. Rushing is a shield. It hides discomfort behind movement. That's why slowing down feels unnatural at first. But the more you practice holding the moment, the more you begin to see what's actually happening inside of it. You start to track your personal programming with more detail. You notice the first flicker of defensiveness before the words come out. You catch the tightening before the judgment forms. This is how rewiring begins — not with a new thought, but with an interrupted pattern.

Over time, the pause becomes your reference point. Not the chaos. Not the reaction. But the still space where you can see both. The moment you realize you have a choice is the moment you stop being owned by your conditioning. This creates a ripple effect. You begin to make different micro-decisions. Not just in moments of conflict, but in subtle, everyday interactions. You speak slower. You choose words more intentionally. You hear people with more accuracy. You act from alignment instead of reactivity.

This isn't about perfection. It's about staying conscious long enough to alter the loop. Even if you miss the pause, even if you react and catch it only afterward, that's still progress. Awareness after the fact is still awareness. And awareness, once built, always moves closer to the moment. Eventually, the gap between trigger and noticing gets smaller. Then one day, you catch it just in time. You pause, hold, breathe — and something shifts. That shift is not always dramatic. Sometimes it's just a softer voice, a slower step, a decision not to send the text. But these small rewires create massive internal momentum. They build a new architecture from the inside out.

You're not just reacting less. You're becoming different. Not artificially, not by suppression, but by reclaiming authorship over how you engage with reality. This is the hidden power of the pause. It doesn't just stop an old pattern. It installs a new one. One that reflects who you are choosing to become, rather than who you were programmed to be.

And the more this becomes natural, the more your external world starts to reflect the internal shift. Environments respond differently. People relate to you differently. Life slows down in the places that once spun out of control. Because now, the power isn't in the event. It's in what you do with it. And that, more than anything else, is what rewires everything.

Part III. The Identity Installation

You've cleared space. You've broken loops. You've rewritten inner responses. Now, we enter the final stage: installation. Not of something foreign, but of something long buried. Your real identity has never been absent. It's been obscured by conditioning, distraction, fear, and repetition. Now it's time to bring it to the surface and install it into the framework of your daily life — consciously, deliberately, and with precision.

Most people try to *achieve* their identity. They chase outcomes, aesthetics, validation. But identity isn't earned through effort. It's revealed through alignment. You don't need to become someone else. You need to *remember* and *install* who you already are beneath the static.

The mistake is thinking that change is something external. That a new job, new partner, new city, or new morning routine will automatically produce a new you. But without internal coherence, those things become costumes. Identity cannot be layered on top of dysfunction. It must emerge from clarity.

This part of the work isn't theoretical. It's applied. It's about encoding the self you've defined into your speech, your actions, your energy, and your presence. It's about making your inner alignment visible, repeatable, and automatic — not because you're performing it, but because you've fused with it. This is what installation really means. Not a one-time choice, but a repeated integration until it becomes reality.

Here, we stop analyzing and start embedding.

We install through decision. Through speech. Through how you respond when no one is watching. Through how you redirect when old impulses try to return. Every moment is an opportunity to choose the self you've now clarified. But this choice must be anchored into the body, not just kept in the mind. Identity must be *lived* before it is believed.

The world responds to coherence. And coherence is only possible when your beliefs, words, and behaviors match. In this part of the system, you'll build that alignment from the ground up. No motivational peaks. No performative highs. Just grounded, unshakable clarity that gets embedded at the level of habit, ritual, and energy. And once it's there, it doesn't need reinforcement. It self-generates.

That's the moment when others notice something has changed. They can't explain it, but they feel it. That's not charisma. That's installation. And it starts now.

Chapter 6: Install the Identity Blueprint

What Identity Really Is and Why You Don't Own Yours Yet

Most people think identity is who they are. But in truth, identity is a program. A composite of inherited language, social imprinting, emotional memory, and neural patterning that tells the story of "I" — not as a fact, but as a loop.

You didn't build your identity. It was assembled. The voice in your head that says "I'm the kind of person who…" is repeating scripts that were installed before you had the awareness to choose. These scripts come from your caregivers, your culture, your traumas, your rewards, and your punishments. And every time you reinforce them — through repetition, emotional reaction, or social validation — you carve the identity loop deeper into your nervous system.

It feels like you. But it's not authored by you.

Think of identity as the sum of your automatic settings. It determines what you expect from yourself, what you allow, what you fear, and what you pursue. It governs how you interpret experience, how you speak to yourself, and what you believe is possible. And because these settings are so familiar, they become invisible. You don't question them. You just operate inside them.

When you say things like "that's just how I am," or "I've always been this way," what you're really saying is: "this is the pattern I haven't questioned yet."

Most identity loops are built for survival, not expansion. They are designed to keep you predictable, manageable, and safe. If you grew up being praised for being smart, you might overidentify with intellect and avoid anything that threatens it. If you were criticized for being emotional, you may have created an identity around being stoic or distant. These adaptations helped you cope once. But they may now be limiting the range of who you're allowed to become.

The danger is that once a pattern gets wrapped in the label of "me," it becomes defended. People will protect the very thing that traps them because losing it feels like death. That's how strong identity attachments are. To the subconscious, change is interpreted as threat. And the deeper the identity structure, the more resistance you'll feel when trying to rewire it.

But here's the truth: identity is not fixed. It is fluid, contextual, and programmable. It can evolve, update, and be re-authored entirely. But only if you're willing to recognize that you didn't truly choose who you are — you inherited who you are supposed to be.

Ownership of identity doesn't come from clinging to your current sense of self. It comes from learning how to shape it consciously.

To do that, you must be able to observe the current construct without defending it. This requires distance. Not disconnection, but awareness. You have to be able to see your thoughts, your tendencies, your default reactions, and your inner language as data — not definitions.

This is where the internal shift begins. You stop assuming that everything you think is true. You stop assuming that everything you feel is final. You begin to study yourself from the outside in and the inside out. Not to judge, but to decode. You learn what has been embedded, what has been copied, what has been distorted, and what has been suppressed.

And slowly, a different voice starts to emerge. One that's not inherited. One that's not reactive. One that doesn't need to prove anything to survive.

That voice will never be loud at first. It won't announce itself with force or confidence. It whispers. It questions gently. It invites you to consider who you could be without the layers of conditioning you've been calling "me." It's in that quiet that the work truly begins...

It's in that quiet that the work truly begins. Not the work of constructing a new persona, but of stripping away what never belonged. When you can pause long enough to hear yourself without the noise of performance, obligation, or fear, you begin to notice the difference between what is *you* and what was merely *installed*.

Real identity ownership requires a dismantling of reflex. It means breaking the automatic links between trigger and response, belief and behavior, expectation and reality. These links make up the architecture of the false self. And because they are so well-rehearsed, they often feel like intuition when they're actually inertia.

This is why growth feels uncomfortable. You're not just learning new ideas. You're confronting old scripts that don't want to die. Every time you act in alignment with a higher version of yourself, your old identity will resist. It will call you fake, dramatic, delusional, selfish. Not because it's true, but because your nervous system thinks familiarity equals safety.

Owning your identity means you don't wait for confirmation. You don't wait for people to agree with the change. You don't need the old system to validate the new one. Instead, you move with clarity, not consensus. You choose what to carry forward and what to leave behind. You decide what patterns get to keep speaking, and which ones get silenced.

You become the editor.

To do this practically, start with language. Words are the access point to self-perception. The way you describe yourself out loud and in your own mind defines the structure of your identity. If you say "I'm always overwhelmed," you reinforce the presence of that loop. If instead you say "I'm learning to respond calmly," you soften the grip of that loop and begin to write a new one.

This is not about lying to yourself. It's about refusing to reinforce what you no longer want to believe. Every sentence is a spell. And the spells you repeat become the reality you live in.

You can also install micro-rituals of redirection. When you catch yourself performing the old identity — the one that seeks approval, stays silent, overworks, self-sabotages, or plays small — pause. Interrupt the behavior, even if it's just with a breath. Then ask: Who am I being right now? Who taught me to be this?

This isn't about shame. It's about sovereignty.

When you build the habit of questioning instead of collapsing, you begin to break the automatic authority of your past. You are no longer just living out an inherited design. You are carving new grooves into your neural pathways. This is identity engineering. Slow. Repetitive. Intentional. But it works.

Eventually, the gap closes. The voice that once whispered becomes louder. Not arrogant, not inflated. Just clear. You begin to feel safe being who you actually are, not who you were rewarded for being. Your choices reflect your values, not your wounds. Your actions become an expression of design, not default.

And that's when identity becomes yours.

Not as a performance, but as a possession. Not as a defense mechanism, but as a living signal. Something you carry with clarity and direction. Something that expands with you, not limits you.

This is the threshold where influence, vision, and magnetism begin to unlock. Because the world doesn't respond to who you pretend to be. It responds to the coherence of someone who knows who they are. Not because they were told, but because they chose.

The Blueprint Model: Self as Code

Most people operate without a conscious blueprint. They respond, react, and adapt, but rarely install. Their sense of self becomes a default program assembled by fragments of experience, expectation, and repetition. This creates an identity not chosen, but inherited. Not designed, but improvised. And that identity, no matter how polished on the surface, keeps looping the same internal code — because it was never authored at the root.

The Blueprint Model begins with a radical premise: that the self is programmable. Not in the mechanical sense, but in the way language, memory, expectation, and emotion combine to form patterns. You are a living system. But like any system, you are shaped by inputs. Your thoughts, your perceptions, your responses — all of these are expressions of an underlying architecture. This architecture is not fixed. It can be rewritten.

This isn't about self-improvement. It's about self-authorship. Improvement assumes something is wrong with you. Authorship recognizes you've simply been running a script that was never yours. A script absorbed from family dynamics, culture, early trauma, or repetition of thought loops. When you begin to see the self as code, you no longer argue with the symptom. You start examining the architecture that creates it.

This is where most transformation efforts fail. They try to change the output without rewriting the codebase. You can motivate yourself to act differently. You can reframe your thoughts or suppress your triggers. But until the blueprint is changed, the old behavior will eventually return. The system will revert. Because it's not the behavior that sustains identity. It's the underlying instructions that run the system in the background.

The subconscious is a builder. It takes the instructions you give it and constructs reality from them. Most of those instructions were planted long ago and have never been audited. If the code says "I must be liked to feel safe," your system will adapt to please. If the code says "Success is dangerous," your behavior will find ways to self-sabotage when you get too close to achievement. These aren't flaws. They are accurate executions of a faulty blueprint.

To change your self-perception, you must alter the source instructions. That means tracing each behavior, response, or pattern back to the internal code that created it. And once identified, that code can be disrupted and rewritten

— not once, but through deliberate repetition, ritual, and reinforcement until the new blueprint becomes the system's default.

This model doesn't require perfection. It requires precision. The question isn't "How can I fix myself?" It's "What instructions is my system following right now?" When you start to notice this, everything becomes data. Every reaction, every internal resistance, every moment of discomfort is not something to fight. It's feedback. It tells you where the blueprint is out of alignment with the identity you are now choosing to install.

This is why the shift into authorship is not emotional. It's structural. Emotional breakthroughs can feel powerful, but without rewiring the underlying architecture, they fade. You go back to who you were, because the blueprint didn't change. The shift must happen at the level where instructions are stored. That's where real identity installation begins.

The subconscious doesn't care if the instructions are helpful or harmful. It only cares about clarity and consistency. This is why many people live in patterns that are painful but familiar. The subconscious will always choose familiarity over unfamiliar freedom, unless a new structure is intentionally installed. Without that structure, the system clings to what is known, because the unknown is coded as unsafe by default.

That's why change often feels like chaos, even when it's good. You're not just altering behavior. You're replacing instructions that once kept you psychologically safe, even if they also kept you stuck. The blueprint isn't emotional, but it is protective. It shields you with code it believes will ensure survival. If the code says, "Don't speak up or you'll lose love," then silence will feel safer than truth. If the code says, "Being different means rejection," then authenticity will always carry the weight of danger. No matter how much you consciously want change, the subconscious will resist if the new behavior violates the existing blueprint.

So you don't fight the resistance. You reprogram it. You identify the line of code that is still running, and you write something new. Not as a one-time declaration, but as a set of layered signals that create safety around the new identity. This is not about brute force. It's about integration. The subconscious accepts new instructions when they come with internal coherence, emotional resonance, and sensory reinforcement. You install the new blueprint the same way the old one was written: through repetition, through emotion, and through embodiment.

This is where precision becomes power. You don't just write a vague affirmation. You write a specific instruction. You don't say "I am powerful" if your subconscious still holds the belief that power leads to rejection. You say, "My power is safe and welcome in the spaces I now choose." That instruction carries precision. It speaks directly to the block. It begins to rewrite the emotional architecture beneath it.

Each micro-upgrade to the code reinforces the system. And the more it aligns with your chosen identity, the less resistance you experience. This is when the subconscious begins to accept the new blueprint not as a threat, but as a truth. It stops defending the old loop, because the new instruction feels equally predictable, equally safe, and more aligned with the life you're building. That's when behavior shifts automatically. That's when thought patterns restructure without struggle.

You're not chasing change. You're writing it. You're not forcing confidence. You're coding it into the structure that defines how you respond to reality. And that's the key: your blueprint doesn't just shape how you see yourself. It filters everything. Every interaction, every opportunity, every failure is processed through the code. Which means that changing the code doesn't just change you — it changes your relationship with reality itself.

This is identity installation in its most powerful form. Not pretending to be someone new, but creating an internal blueprint that makes that version of you inevitable. Not through force, but through design. And once the system is stable, once the new instructions are clear, your subconscious will begin to build from them without hesitation. Because that's what it's always done. It builds what it's told.

You are not at the mercy of your programming. You are its architect. The code is not sacred. It's editable. The self is not fixed. It's adaptive. And the life that feels out of reach isn't waiting for the perfect version of you. It's waiting for the precise instructions that allow the current version of you to evolve into the next. Now you know where to write them.

Override Your Operating System

Every system runs on a set of rules. Your mind is no different. What you think of as personality, preference, or habit is often just software installed over time. Code written by repetition, emotion, environment, and survival logic. Most people never question this system. They live their entire lives reacting to inputs based on pre-written outputs, unaware that what feels like a choice is often just automation.

This is your operating system: the subconscious logic that filters reality, interprets data, and generates behavior. It's not malicious. It's efficient. It's designed to reduce cognitive load by running predetermined sequences, allowing you to act quickly and predictably in familiar situations. But what happens when the familiar is no longer useful? When the automatic behavior keeps creating results you don't want?

That's when the system must be overridden. Not destroyed. Not fought. Overridden. Because the truth is, your current operating system was built to protect you, not to empower you. It was designed for safety, not expansion. Every limiting behavior or belief has roots in perceived threat or discomfort. Avoidance, hesitation, procrastination — they're not personality flaws. They're the outputs of a protective system that hasn't been updated.

And here's what most people don't realize: the operating system isn't fixed. It's adaptive. It just responds to whatever is repeated with enough clarity and emotional intensity. But unless you consciously install new logic, the system will keep running old code indefinitely. Not because it's broken. Because it's loyal.

This loyalty is the barrier and the key. The system is loyal to whatever feels most known. That's why it clings to patterns that feel safe, even if they're self-sabotaging. It resists change not because change is bad, but because uncertainty is coded as danger. This is not rational fear. It's primitive programming. The subconscious doesn't evaluate potential. It recognizes patterns. And it protects what it knows.

So the goal is not to fight the old system. It's to feed the new one. And that begins with awareness: seeing your behavior not as who you are, but as what you've been running. This shift is subtle but radical. Instead of saying "I'm indecisive," you recognize "I've been running a pattern of indecision." That single shift turns a fixed identity into editable code.

Once you see it, you can start rewriting. But don't expect the system to yield instantly. Override requires repetition. It requires you to introduce new inputs until the outputs begin to shift on their own. This is the heart of reprogramming: consistency over time, layered with intention and clarity.

One of the most powerful ways to override the system is through what we could call frictional awareness. The moment you notice a default response kicking in — an urge to self-sabotage, withdraw, lash out, stay silent — you interrupt the sequence. Not with shame, not with force, but with a pause. A moment of deliberate presence. You bring your attention to the surface layer of the code, and you choose a different instruction.

This choice is where override begins. It's not a grand reinvention. It's a micro-intervention. A moment where you remember: the system is running you, but you are not the system. You can act from it, or you can act beyond it.

That choice — repeated and reinforced — becomes the new instruction. It starts to encode itself into the deeper layers of your mind, until what once felt unfamiliar begins to feel normal. And that is the tipping point: when the override becomes the new default.

The new default doesn't arrive with a bang. It arrives quietly, often unnoticed. One day, you respond differently, and it doesn't feel like effort. You didn't have to battle the urge. You just didn't run the old code. That's when you know the override is no longer a conscious effort. It has become the system.

This is where most people give up too early. They expect the override to be a sudden, dramatic shift. But systems don't change through intensity alone. They change through precision, repetition, and stability. The brain rewires itself not through explosions of motivation, but through patterned inputs delivered over time. Your system will always reflect what it has been taught to normalize.

So if your system has normalized conflict avoidance, people-pleasing, self-censorship, or waiting for permission, it will not suddenly shift just because you understand why it exists. Understanding is important, but it doesn't rewrite the code. Repetition does. This is why awareness without application creates frustration. You can see the glitch, but unless you act against it, you keep feeding the same instruction loop.

And there's something else to consider: the override will feel uncomfortable before it feels powerful. The system interprets anything unfamiliar as unstable. Choosing a new pattern won't feel natural at first. It will feel like friction. That friction is not failure. It's a sign that you are operating at the edge of your existing code. It's the signal that you are stepping into conscious authorship.

But conscious authorship demands consistency. If you show up once, the system sees it as noise. If you show up again and again with clarity and emotional precision, the system begins to adapt. It doesn't resist out of malice. It resists to test for coherence. Are you serious? Are you consistent? Is this signal safe enough to become the new norm?

This is the subconscious contract. It will upgrade the code if the new input is stable enough to protect the system. That's your job — not to demand change, but to create stability in the override. To choose the new instruction often enough that it becomes safer than the old one.

This is why emotional charge matters. When you install new instructions in a high-emotion state, they embed faster. That's why breakthroughs in moments of clarity or anger or joy can become turning points. But you can't rely on emotion alone. Emotion sparks the override. Repetition cements it. The real magic happens in the small, unglamorous moments. The breath before a reaction. The choice to respond, not reflexively, but deliberately. The decision to pause instead of retreat. To speak truth instead of playing a role. These are not random acts. They are rewrites. Every one of them carves a new neural path. Every one of them teaches the system: this is who we are now.

And it's not about perfection. Some days, you'll run the old code. That's not failure. That's data. It's a chance to see which part of the system is still anchored to survival logic. And from there, you go again. You bring consciousness back into the sequence. You remember you are the operator, not the operation.

Eventually, you stop needing to override. The system runs your new code by default. But even then, mastery means staying awake. You don't fall asleep at the wheel just because you built a better vehicle. You stay aware. You fine-tune. You keep your system clean, agile, and aligned with who you are becoming.

Because ultimately, override is not about rebellion. It's about authorship. It's about reclaiming the right to run your own code, in a world that constantly tries to install its own. When you do that consistently, you don't just change behavior. You change identity. And that shift is permanent. Not because it was forced, but because it was chosen.

Chapter 7: Activate the Influence Protocol

Reprogramming Your Signal: The Hidden Layer of Influence

There's a layer of influence that precedes language, precedes action, and even precedes thought. It is the signal you emit — the composite of your energy, intention, and subconscious posture. People respond to this signal long before they respond to your words. It's not mystical. It's pattern recognition. At a subconscious level, the human nervous system is wired to detect what is safe, what is credible, and what is dominant. This detection happens in milliseconds. It bypasses logic. And it makes most persuasion techniques irrelevant if your signal contradicts your words.

This is why some people can walk into a room and shift its energy without saying a word, while others need to shout to be heard and still get ignored. The difference is not volume. The difference is signal integrity. The external world mirrors the internal frequency you're broadcasting, whether you are aware of it or not. So if you're trying to build authority, connection, or magnetism without first rewriting the signal you're sending, you're playing the influence game with broken code.

The signal is not about image. It's not posture in the superficial sense. You can fake confidence in your voice, mimic power in your body language, or rehearse lines from a book on charisma, but if your internal signal still carries unresolved fear, doubt, or need, people will feel it. This is not about manipulation. It's about congruence. Influence flows naturally when the external matches the internal.

So how do you reprogram your signal? It starts with understanding that your signal is built from the instructions your nervous system has received and repeated over time. If you were taught that speaking up led to rejection, your signal likely broadcasts contraction. If your survival once depended on being invisible, your signal may now default to energetic smallness, even if your words are bold. These old programs continue to broadcast beneath your conscious behavior. Until they are rewritten, your influence will always be capped by your signal.

Reprogramming requires interrupting the loop between unconscious expectation and embodied transmission. Your body is not just a container. It is an antenna. It transmits everything you believe to be true about your value, your place, and your power. And it does so whether or not you speak. So the work begins not with the mind, but with the body. Not with words, but with presence.

One of the fastest ways to detect your current signal is to observe how people respond to you when you are not actively performing. Not when you're trying to impress, but when you're simply being. Do people defer to your energy or dominate it? Do they open up or close off? Do they feel pulled toward you or slightly off balance in your presence? This reflection tells you what you're transmitting.

The next step is not to change how others react, but to change what you're sending out in the first place. That means shifting from reactive posture to generative posture — from responding to old patterns to broadcasting a new frequency based on conscious identity, not inherited programming.

This begins with internal recalibration. Before you walk into the room. Before you speak. Before you strategize. You decide what signal you're going to run. And not just in concept, but in sensation. This is not about pretending. It's about remembering. You don't create a signal by forcing confidence. You access the signal that aligns with your highest coherence. You embody the state that reflects the identity you've chosen.

This internal alignment becomes the new instruction the body follows. And when the body broadcasts that signal with enough consistency, people respond differently — not because you said something clever, but because your presence gave them no choice.

Most people unconsciously wait for permission from their environment to feel powerful, grounded, or safe. They scan for cues before deciding who to be. That's reactive wiring. And it keeps their signal unstable. One day they feel confident because they were validated. The next, they collapse because the validation didn't arrive. The nervous system becomes a puppet of feedback. But true influence begins when you stop waiting for the external world to reflect back your worth and instead decide to install it as your default transmission.

This is not a mental decision alone. It must be installed through repetition in the body. If the nervous system has spent years contracting in response to perceived threat — social rejection, judgment, disapproval — then those pathways must be disrupted through deliberate signal practice. It's not about affirmations. It's about becoming fluent in a new energetic language.

This is where intentional embodiment practices come in. The nervous system learns through sensation and experience, not logic. If you want to broadcast certainty, your body must first learn what certainty feels like as a baseline. If you want to radiate calm authority, you must train your system to hold that frequency in real time, especially under pressure. Otherwise, the moment you're tested, the old signal returns.

Signal training doesn't require theatrics. It doesn't require pretending to be someone else. It requires stillness, presence, and deliberate state access. You learn to drop into the frequency you choose to run. You practice holding it. You stay with it longer than your impulse to shrink, appease, or perform. And when your body wants to default back into familiar contraction, you override the impulse with awareness instead of habit.

The longer you hold the new frequency, the more stable the transmission becomes. This stability is what people feel when they sense someone has a strong presence. It's not magic. It's internal consistency. The nervous system is no longer leaking energy or broadcasting doubt. It's transmitting a signal that others can sync with.

This is why some people seem to generate trust, attraction, or deference effortlessly. Their signal is clean. It doesn't contradict itself. There's no gap between what they say and what they emanate. And because humans are wired to tune into consistency, people lean into what feels energetically coherent, often without realizing it.

If your signal is confused, your influence will be inconsistent. You may have moments of clarity, but they won't last. That's because your body hasn't integrated the new code as a stable default. It still references the old instructions. So every time you're under stress, it reverts.

To break this cycle, you must anchor the new signal even deeper than your reactions. You make it your set point. You install it as the silent broadcast of your being. Not to manipulate others, but to live in alignment with the frequency of your chosen self. That alignment is the hidden lever of influence. It shapes perception before perception has a chance to form. It guides interaction before a word is spoken.

This is the layer that most never access, not because it's difficult, but because it requires patience, presence, and radical self-awareness. You don't reprogram your signal once. You tune it daily. You train your system to hold it across contexts. And over time, the outside world catches up. People begin to respond not to your efforts, but to your essence. Not to your strategies, but to your stability.

The greatest influence doesn't come from force. It comes from frequency. When your signal is clean, congruent, and embodied, it moves the world around you without effort. And that is the real code behind unseen power.

Embody the Frame: Reality Responds to You

Most people live inside someone else's frame. They walk into a room and scan for dominant energy. They absorb the loudest tone, the sharpest look, or the most confident posture, then recalibrate who they are in response to it. This is what it means to live inside external permission. It's an unconscious submission to frames that feel more certain than their own.

But here's the hidden truth: the most powerful person in the room is never the loudest. It's the one who holds their frame without blinking. The one who doesn't flinch under pressure. The one whose sense of reality is so internally consistent that it bends the space around it.

This is not charisma. It's not confidence as a surface performance. It's frame embodiment. And it's a choice.

To understand this, you have to see the frame not as an idea, but as a living field. A frame is not just what you believe. It's what you radiate. It's the energetic boundary that defines what is real for you and what is not. And when that boundary is held with conviction, the environment adjusts to it.

This is what happens when someone walks into a situation and, without saying much, everything subtly shifts. People begin to listen more closely. Conversations slow down. Tension in the air gets recalibrated. That's not luck or social dominance. It's the result of someone who has chosen their frame and refuses to outsource it.

To embody the frame, you must decide that your internal reality has more authority than any external cue. That doesn't mean ignoring input. It means filtering input through the lens of what you have already chosen to hold as true.

This requires inner congruence. If you doubt your own perspective, your frame collapses the moment it's challenged. If you posture, but don't believe what you're broadcasting, your frame will fracture. And others will sense it. People are wired to detect inconsistency, even if they don't consciously know what they're picking up on.

Frame embodiment, then, is not about dominance. It's about integrity. The integrity of thought, energy, and presence. When you live inside your own frame without needing to prove it, defend it, or inflate it, you become the gravitational center of your environment. Not because you try to be, but because the field around you picks up the signal and recalibrates.

But this only works if you've actually chosen a frame worth holding.

If you're operating from reactive identity, where your beliefs and self-perception are shaped by avoidance, trauma, or inherited patterns, then the frame you're reinforcing is not truly yours. It might have the illusion of strength, but it will always carry the underlying energy of survival. And survival-based frames are brittle. They might hold for a while, but the moment they're no longer useful for protection, they fall apart.

To hold a real frame, you must source it from clarity, not compensation. It must come from knowing who you are, not from needing to be seen a certain way. That's what gives it density. That's what makes it unshakable when tested.

You've seen this before. The person who walks away from an argument not because they're afraid to fight, but because the argument doesn't register as relevant to their world. The entrepreneur who doesn't panic during a setback because they've already integrated chaos into their success blueprint. The leader who doesn't chase validation because their signal is already calibrated to internal approval.

These are not personalities. These are people who have chosen and trained their frame. And the world bends toward them accordingly.

Now the question becomes: what frame are you currently holding? And does it actually reflect your chosen self — or just your historical self?

If your frame is outdated, reactive, or fragmented, the environment around you reflects it with equal distortion. You might attract instability, misalignment, or resistance—not because you are cursed or unlucky, but because your signal is unclear. You haven't defined the rules of your reality, so external inputs default to noise. You get pulled by strong personalities. You doubt your intuition when it's quiet. You question your worth in moments of tension. This is not weakness. It's the result of not installing the frame that belongs to you.

Reclaiming it doesn't require a dramatic transformation. It begins with internal enforcement. If you don't hold your frame, it dissolves. And if it dissolves, something else rushes in to replace it—usually something that benefits someone else. That's how influence works. The one with the stronger energetic frame writes the rules of the interaction. And the one who needs to be validated loses authorship of their experience.

To regain control, you must decide that your perception matters more than reaction. Your inner narrative must take precedence over external signals, even when they're loud. Especially when they're loud. Because the louder the outside gets, the more you're being tested for alignment. Most people flinch when this happens. They interpret intensity as danger and shrink their frame. But the ones who hold it see pressure as the forge. They welcome the heat because they know what's being sculpted underneath.

To get to this level, embodiment must go beyond thought. You can't mentally convince yourself into frame authority. You have to live it. You have to carry it in your voice when you speak to yourself. In your spine when you walk into the room. In your choices when you're unseen, and no one's watching.

Frame is frequency. People don't respond to your words. They respond to the calibration underneath them. You can say all the right things, but if your energy is inconsistent or unsure, the deeper signal dominates. This is why manipulation tactics eventually collapse. You can fake language, but you can't fake signal for long. Eventually, reality picks up the deeper layer and mirrors it back. You can't hide from what you actually hold.

When your frame is integrated, there is no posturing. There is no inflation. There is only congruence. Your presence becomes more influential not because you are trying to influence, but because there is nothing misaligned to push against. People relax around embodied energy. They orient to it. Not out of submission, but resonance. It feels safe, not because it's soft, but because it's stable. In a world built on volatility, stability becomes magnetic. This is also why people with true frame don't chase outcomes. They don't need to control every detail, because they've already calibrated their internal environment. They trust that reality will mirror that structure back. Not in a mystical or passive way, but because energy tends to organize itself around clarity. What is clear and consistent becomes the anchor point for everything else.

There is no shortcut to this. Frame embodiment is a daily practice. Not a grind, but a discipline. It requires you to notice where your frame leaks. Where you speak from insecurity, or shrink to fit comfort. Where you seek proof before conviction, instead of holding conviction and letting reality catch up. These micro-moments are not trivial. They are training. Every time you hold your internal standard without flinching, you reinforce the signal. Every time you correct your posture, your tone, your mental loop—

without collapsing into emotion—you teach your body that your frame is safe to hold.

Eventually, it becomes effortless. Not because it's easy, but because it becomes you. You stop performing strength and start radiating it. You no longer need to be louder than the noise, because the noise no longer has authority.

This is what it means to be the frame. It's not a concept. It's a way of being that alters how the world responds to you—not through force, but through frequency. Not through dominance, but through deep, silent certainty. That's the real power. And once you embody it, you never give it back.

Install the Internal Mirror Script

Before anything shifts on the outside, it must first be rewritten on the inside. Your subconscious does not operate based on what is happening externally. It operates based on what it hears most consistently within. The internal script is the invisible prompt feeding your identity, your actions, and your results. If you've been stuck, reactive, insecure, or looping in the same patterns, it's not because you lack power. It's because your internal narrator has been running an outdated program—and no one ever showed you how to rewrite it.

This is the internal mirror script. It's the voice that tells you who you are and what's possible. It is not your thoughts. It is the layer behind your thoughts. And more importantly, it is programmable. Not in a fake, forced affirmation kind of way, but in a deeply biological and behavioral way. Your nervous system organizes around what it hears repeatedly. Your perception of reality will follow whatever story gets installed the most. This is not psychological fluff. It's survival-level logic. If the internal voice says "I am unsafe," your mind will scan for threats. If it says "I am invisible," your body will shrink before the room even sees you. And if it says "I always lose," your decisions will be shaped to match that outcome without needing your conscious permission.

This is why transformation begins with the mirror script. Before any goal becomes real, before any influence gets activated, you must confront the source code that runs underneath your behavior. The part of you that speaks in silence. That defines worth without needing language. That repeats the same internal sentence until it becomes a prediction.

The mirror script you carry right now was not born from truth. It was assembled through repetition. Maybe it came from childhood, from early rejection, from unmet expectations, from a traumatic rupture or a slow erosion over time. Wherever it came from, it does not need to stay. But you do have to replace it intentionally. You cannot simply "think differently." The mirror script only rewrites when new language meets consistent action. Identity does not change because you want it to. It changes when your nervous system sees that a new sentence gets backed by actual evidence.

To begin, you must become aware of the dominant phrases that currently run your internal world. Not surface thoughts, but the deeper assumptions. The ones that show up when you are alone, triggered, or uncertain. These are the ones that dictate your posture, your voice tone, your social energy, your attraction patterns, your leadership capacity. They are subtle, but they are running everything.

Start by catching them mid-loop. The moment your body tightens or you feel a drop in certainty, ask: "What did I just say to myself without realizing it?" The answer might be something like "I'm messing this up," "I'm too much," "They don't respect me," or "I'll never change." These phrases may seem small, but they build a self-image over time that becomes hard to argue with. Not because they are true, but because they go unchallenged.

Your job is not to fight the old sentence. That only strengthens it. Your job is to install a new one and back it with action until the nervous system recognizes it as valid. This does not mean repeating fluffy affirmations. It means giving yourself a command that you can actually embody. Something true enough to believe, yet powerful enough to move the system forward.

The real test of your internal mirror script isn't found in calm moments. It's found when the heat rises. When the outcome is uncertain. When you're misunderstood, doubted, rejected, or left out. That's when the original sentence comes back to reclaim its territory. It doesn't shout. It slips in through your posture, your hesitation, the tension behind your smile. In those moments, you're not just dealing with a reaction. You're witnessing an identity defaulting to script.

This is why rewriting the mirror script isn't just about morning practices or journal entries. It's about embedding new language directly into the emotional core of your day. You are not just shifting thoughts. You are training your nervous system to recognize a new code as normal.

Start small. Begin with one moment a day that you consciously choose to override. Pick a scenario that would normally trigger self-doubt or reactivity. In that moment, when the familiar pattern starts to play, speak the new script with intention. Not to convince yourself, but to interrupt the automation. Say it clearly. Say it out loud if you can. And follow it with a single action that aligns with the new sentence.

If your original mirror script says, "I'm not taken seriously," your override might sound like, "My voice holds weight." Then you say the thing you were going to hold back. You don't wait for the room to agree. You embody it before there's proof.

The mirror begins to change the moment the internal sentence is backed by a bold, congruent move. It doesn't have to be dramatic. Just real. Just anchored. Identity isn't about volume. It's about alignment. When your words and actions speak the same language, the system listens.

There's also a deeper layer here. As you begin to install new scripts, you'll feel resistance. Not because the sentence is wrong, but because the body is addicted to the emotional signature of the old one. If your identity has been shaped through stress, guilt, or rejection, then peace and power will feel foreign at first. That's expected. You are not failing. You are detoxing from a false identity.

It's crucial that you stay with the new script long enough for the nervous system to stop flagging it as a threat. Repetition here is not about forcing a belief. It's about building familiarity. The more often your system hears a sentence that reflects your power, the less it needs to prepare for collapse. Eventually, the override becomes the default. And you don't need to repeat it anymore because your actions already do.

This process is not about becoming someone new. It's about removing the noise that has kept you from hearing your original signal. The one you had before the world taught you who to be. The mirror script isn't just a self-talk technique. It's a reactivation of your actual code.

As this rewiring deepens, you'll begin to notice that certain people, environments, and dynamics no longer resonate. Not because they changed, but because your internal reflection no longer matches their frequency. This is a sign that the mirror is no longer fractured. You've stopped arguing for the limitations that once felt like truth. You've stopped echoing a story that was never yours to carry.

And the most powerful part is that you didn't do it through force. You did it through precision. You chose a sentence. You embodied it. You made it real. Not because the world gave you permission, but because you reclaimed your own.

That's how internal reality reshapes the external world. One sentence at a time, backed by one aligned action at a time, until who you are becomes undeniable. Even in silence. Even in chaos. Even when no one else sees it yet. Because by then, your mirror already does.

Chapter 8: Collapse the Old Self

Why Growth Feels Draining: Identity Conflict

You've likely been told that growth is hard, that transformation demands effort, sacrifice, discomfort. And that's partially true. But what no one explains is why it often feels so *draining*. Not just difficult, but *exhausting*. Like trying to sprint with a parachute strapped to your back. You take the steps. You read the books. You do the work. And yet, something inside seems to pull against it. Not with words, but with fatigue. Resistance disguised as tiredness. As overthinking. As collapse.

This isn't laziness. It's identity conflict.

When you attempt to grow without updating the identity that anchors your behavior, your system goes into friction mode. You're pushing forward with new thoughts, new habits, maybe even new environments. But internally, the operating definition of "who I am" hasn't shifted. And your nervous system interprets anything that contradicts that definition as a potential threat.

It's not your fault. The brain is designed for efficiency, not evolution. It wants to conserve energy. And identity is one of the most efficient mechanisms it uses. The "I" you believe yourself to be is not just an abstract sense of self. It's a bundle of stories, emotional setpoints, social roles, and behavioral patterns that have been rehearsed for years, often unconsciously. This bundle creates a psychological center of gravity. And no matter how strong your desire for change, you'll always be pulled back toward it until that gravitational point is deliberately adjusted.

This is where the drain begins.

Every time you try to step beyond your old identity—whether it's starting a business, setting a boundary, changing your routine, or stepping into leadership—you're asking your system to behave as someone you haven't fully integrated yet. It's not that the new version of you is inauthentic. It's just not *installed* yet. So the system flags it. It questions your right to act like that. It demands proof that it's safe. And when it doesn't get that proof immediately, it activates stress.

That stress shows up as indecision, mental fatigue, or emotional shutdown. You're not broken. You're experiencing *split allegiance*. One part of you wants the expansion. Another part still feels loyal to the identity that's being left behind. And that loyalty runs deep.

You see, the old identity wasn't just comfortable. It was familiar. Even if it was rooted in limitation, it came with a sense of known territory. You knew how to exist inside it. You knew what to expect. You knew the emotional baseline. You even knew what kind of relationships fit inside that self-image. So when you start to stretch beyond it, you're not just disrupting patterns—you're threatening entire systems of belonging, coping, and meaning.

Your fatigue isn't weakness. It's feedback.

It's your nervous system asking for coherence. For alignment between your internal blueprint and your external behavior. Until that alignment is there, growth will always feel heavier than it needs to be. You'll be dragging the weight of an outdated self behind every decision, every risk, every step into the unfamiliar.

This is why affirmations, motivation, or even discipline often fall short. They don't resolve the root tension. They only layer new behavior on top of an old script. And unless that script is rewritten at the identity level, your growth will feel like resistance training without rest. You'll keep burning energy trying to hold two realities at once: the one you're stepping into and the one you haven't let go of yet.

The turning point comes when you stop trying to *force* growth and begin to *integrate* it. That means recognizing that your internal system is not resisting because it hates progress. It's resisting because it has not been reassured that this new way of being is safe, consistent, and emotionally congruent. You have to become the kind of person your system believes in—not because of willpower, but because of internal logic.

To do this, the identity itself must evolve. And identity is not changed by declarations. It is changed through evidence. You must give your nervous system real proof that this new version of you is stable, coherent, and familiar enough to become the new baseline. Until then, it will treat every bold move as a temporary anomaly or a threat to self-preservation.

This is why the exhaustion hits hardest in the early phases of personal transformation. You are in a liminal space: no longer who you used to be, but not yet stabilized as who you're becoming. You are shedding old emotional setpoints and behavioral patterns, but the replacement software hasn't fully embedded. So everything takes more energy. Every choice, every interaction, every piece of expression. It's all filtered through a system that's still scanning for danger, confusion, or loss.

Loss, especially, is underestimated. You're not just growing. You're grieving. Even when the old identity was filled with pain, it still held meaning. Letting go of it can feel like betraying the younger version of you who needed that survival strategy. It can feel like saying goodbye to a familiar emotional rhythm, or stepping outside of a group dynamic that once felt like home. That emotional cost is real. It's why people sabotage their own evolution. Not because they're weak, but because they haven't been taught how to close the gap between expansion and integration.

So what does that closing of the gap actually look like?

It starts with conscious reinforcement. You begin living as if the new identity is already trusted by your system. Not to perform it, but to *rehearse* it. You show up as the new frame long enough, consistently enough, and gently enough that the body no longer reacts with alarm. You don't rush it. You train it. Like teaching a new language to a child. You speak it. You repeat it. You embody it even when the feedback is slow.

The body learns through felt experience. This means your emotions have to feel the shift—not just your mind. You create environments, rituals, and relationships that mirror the new self until they become default. Not because you're faking it, but because you are anchoring it. Identity conflict dissolves not when you *decide* who you are, but when your whole system stops questioning it.

This is not about abandoning who you were. It's about reassigning the narrative. You're not erasing the past. You're upgrading the function. What used to be a survival script becomes a reference point—not a command center. And as the old self relaxes its grip, the drain begins to disappear. Energy that was once spent in internal friction becomes available for direction, clarity, and presence.

You'll know you're integrating when growth no longer feels like struggle. It may still be challenging, but it won't feel like self-betrayal. You won't be fighting your own wiring every time you speak with power, claim a boundary, or walk away from an old pattern. Your nervous system won't flinch. It will recognize the signal. It will align with it. And that alignment is what turns growth from something exhausting into something exhilarating. There is no shortcut to this. But there is a path. You're already on it. Now it's time to stop dragging your old self behind you and start stepping fully into the one your system is ready to believe. When that shift lands, growth stops draining you. It starts fueling you.

The Collapse Ritual: Burning the Previous Version

You cannot code a new identity into a system still haunted by the ghost of who you used to be. The subconscious clings to the familiar, even when the familiar is broken. And while most people try to install a new self on top of the old one, real transformation only stabilizes when the old scaffolding is dismantled. This is why the collapse ritual matters. Not symbolically. Functionally.

The previous version of you was built out of necessity. Every pattern, every behavior, every mask you wore was crafted to survive something. Maybe it was to fit into a family system, to avoid punishment, to receive approval, to avoid abandonment. These layers weren't mistakes. They were strategies. You didn't become that version out of failure. You became it because your system believed it was the best way to stay safe, seen, or in control.

But what once protected you eventually imprisons you.

You feel it when your voice goes quiet in moments that require power. When your posture collapses under scrutiny. When you pull back just before the breakthrough. That's not just fear. It's the echo of an outdated identity. And it won't leave just because you want it to. It will only release when you consciously end its contract.

This is where most people hesitate. They assume that change is additive. That if they just read enough, train enough, meditate enough, they'll eventually become someone new. But no amount of addition will override a foundation that hasn't been cleared. You don't just become. You *unbecome* first. And this process is not always clean or pleasant. It often involves a collapse.

The collapse is not chaos. It is release. It is the disintegration of the identity that no longer serves you. But because that identity was tied to emotional survival, the collapse can feel like death. That's why it must be made conscious. Ritualized. Not performed for others, but claimed internally as an act of final severance.

The ritual doesn't need to be elaborate, but it does need to be embodied. You are telling your system: "This is the end of that script. It is no longer needed. I choose something new." Without this conscious severance, the nervous system keeps checking for the old code. It wonders if the former self might return. And so it delays full integration of the new one.

This is why journaling alone doesn't cut it. Talking about your transformation is not the same as sealing it. The mind loves to talk. It will script a thousand versions of who you want to be. But until the body believes that the former self is truly gone, it will stay half-committed, half-engaged, and half-alive.

That inner halfway point is what creates the worst kind of fatigue. You're trying to carry the energy of becoming while still dragging the remnants of what you used to be. You step into a new habit, but the old identity whispers. You speak a new truth, but the former version flinches. That tension isn't failure. It's just unresolved transition. And it's a call for closure. What you are about to learn is not just a metaphorical practice. It is a signal. A line in the sand. It tells your system: "This version of me ends here." And once the system accepts that message, space opens. Energy returns. And the new operating identity can actually begin to function without resistance.

To execute this properly, you must move beyond symbolic gestures and into cellular conviction. Your system must feel that something real has ended. This requires honesty. You have to face what the previous version of you protected, what it avoided, and what it tolerated. You need to name it, without judgment. Not to shame it, but to complete it.

Completion is the medicine. Not suppression. Not bypassing. When something is complete, it no longer repeats. That's how you remove the energetic loop that keeps trying to run in the background. And this is the purpose of the collapse ritual: to bring everything that version of you carried to a final moment of truth.

If you've ever had a moment of deep grief, you already know the feeling. The breath shifts. The body softens. The nervous system finally stops bracing. That's when release happens. The collapse ritual mimics this pattern consciously. Instead of waiting for breakdowns to force your release, you bring it forward intentionally.

You can write the obituary of the former self. You can list out its beliefs, its behaviors, its fears. You can burn the pages, bury the object, or speak the words aloud in solitude. The specific action is secondary to the emotional truth behind it. What matters is that the gesture comes from your core. This is not performance. It's internal declaration.

When done correctly, something strange tends to happen. A sense of emptiness shows up. Not the painful kind, but the quiet kind. The space that opens when noise dies. The pause that signals: it's done. For many, this feels disorienting. You might even feel unmotivated, blank, or unsure. This is not regression. It's the recalibration that follows energetic severance.

In this space, your system is no longer reacting from the past, but it hasn't yet been given the full blueprint of the new identity. It's in a state of readiness. A void with intelligence. This is the most fertile ground you'll ever stand on. And how you respond to this space determines what installs next. If you rush to fill it with distractions, old behaviors can sneak back in. The subconscious doesn't care if a pattern is outdated, as long as it feels familiar. It will resurrect the script if you don't hold the silence long enough for something truer to take root. This is why most personal development efforts relapse. People remove one mask and instantly reach for another. The collapse ritual must be followed by stillness.

Let the void breathe for a moment. Let your nervous system taste what it's like to not be any version at all. This is where your authority returns. From here, identity is no longer reactive. It becomes authored.

Only then can you consciously build the self you actually choose.

That's the point of all this. You're not trying to become someone else. You're reclaiming authorship over your own programming. And until you remove the false authorship—the societal scripts, the inherited beliefs, the fear-based constructs—you're just editing someone else's code.

You collapse the previous version not because it was bad, but because it was never truly yours.

Once it's gone, you are left with pure signal. Not noise. Not confusion. Just the raw truth of what you are when nothing is performing for approval. From that place, clarity rises on its own. Direction becomes obvious. You don't need to force motivation. You simply act, because your actions are no longer filtered through distortion.

This is the difference between incremental change and core transformation. One tweaks the symptoms. The other rewrites the source.

The collapse is the gate. You walk through it alone. But on the other side, the energy you've been waiting for finally arrives. Not because you chased it, but because you made room for it.

Burn what was. Mean it. And watch what you become.

Reclaim the Energy From the Mental Past

Most people are exhausted, not because of what they are doing, but because of what they are carrying. Mental fatigue rarely comes from the present moment. It comes from the past trying to stay alive in the present. Every unprocessed experience, unfinished narrative, and unresolved identity quietly demands energy to remain active. These fragments operate like open tabs in a browser. One or two don't cause problems. But hundreds, running all at once, slow down the system. Eventually, it crashes.

You don't need to have lived through intense trauma to be drained by the past. Even subtle loops, like regretting a conversation, resenting an old version of yourself, or mentally replaying what you "should have done," are enough to deplete your mental clarity. And it's not just the memory itself that pulls on your energy. It's the identity you built around that memory. The internal meaning assigned to it. The emotional posture you've held onto since then.

You might be living in a completely different environment now, but if your nervous system is still patterned to protect against something that happened five years ago, that event is still present for your body. This is why people feel stuck even when life looks "fine" on paper. They have energy leaks. And those leaks are tied to mental residue that has never been neutralized.

Reclaiming energy from the past doesn't mean forgetting it. It means completing it. Completion doesn't always require forgiveness. It doesn't always require confrontation. What it does require is a decision: this part of my story is no longer active in my system. That decision, made consciously, begins the withdrawal of your energy from the outdated neural loop.

To do this, you need to bring awareness to where your energy is still entangled. Start by noticing which past memories you still react to, even slightly. The memories that still tighten your chest, make your stomach sink, or pull your thoughts into spirals. These are signals. They indicate that the moment has not ended within you, even if it ended externally long ago.

Sometimes, the mind doesn't let go of the past because it feels unresolved. And it often feels unresolved because you never got the version of the ending you wanted. Maybe you wanted justice. Or closure. Or validation. And because that didn't come, you keep mentally revisiting the situation, as if you can edit it from the present. But you can't. The past isn't a live document. It's a snapshot. And every time you revisit it hoping to rewrite it, you actually reinforce the version that originally hurt you.

This is one of the most draining dynamics the human system can fall into. Mental time travel with no resolution. Living in a constant tug-of-war between what happened and what should have happened. Your energy gets pulled into the gap. And that energy is vital. It's the same energy you need to create, to feel present, to act in alignment. When it's hijacked by the past, you become slow to respond, quick to doubt, and prone to overthinking.

You might find yourself procrastinating, not because you're lazy, but because your inner space is crowded. You're trying to act in the present while filtering reality through a stack of outdated frames. No matter how sharp your goals are, you won't be able to execute with clarity until you clear the distortion. You can't channel full focus through a fogged lens.

You cannot force yourself to let go of the past, but you can withdraw your participation from it. The key is to stop feeding it. That doesn't mean ignoring it. It means interrupting the emotional reinforcement loop that gives it power. Every time you mentally revisit an old story and assign it the same meaning, you anchor it deeper. The only way to dislodge it is by neutralizing its emotional charge and creating a new context around it.

One way to do this is to mentally separate the experience from the identity it created. When something painful happens, the mind not only records the event, it also builds a meaning structure around it. That structure might sound like: "I'm not good enough," "People always betray me," or "I can't trust anyone." These aren't just thoughts. They're energetic conclusions your nervous system accepted. To reclaim energy, you need to break these conclusions. And that doesn't require digging into the past. It requires confronting the current identity that's still acting on those conclusions.

Ask yourself: what part of me is still protecting an outdated story? What do I believe I need to guard against? What survival strategy am I still running that no longer applies to the life I live now?

Sometimes it helps to speak directly to the version of you that lived through the moment. Imagine them standing in front of you. Let yourself acknowledge the truth of what they felt. Not from a place of victimhood, but from compassion. Tell them the part of the story they never heard. The part that brings completion. Maybe it's as simple as: "You're not stuck there anymore. You're safe now. I've got it from here."

This process is not about pretending nothing happened. It's about removing the frozen imprint from your inner space. Most people carry an internal museum of emotional artifacts that they never revisit intentionally, but which shape their behavior in the background. That museum keeps you heavy. If you want freedom, you must choose to stop being the curator of what no longer defines you.

There is a mental discipline required to do this. You will have to interrupt the reflex to keep narrating old pain. You will have to notice when you slip into old interpretations and deliberately refuse to follow them. This doesn't mean suppressing your truth. It means no longer submitting to the version of reality that disempowers you.

Clarity returns when the channel is clear. When you release the outdated story, your nervous system recalibrates. The constant background tension lifts. You'll notice you can breathe deeper. You'll move through your day without that familiar inner resistance. You'll stop questioning whether you're enough, whether you belong, or whether you're ready. You'll simply act. You'll simply be.

And what was once draining becomes fuel. Not because you rewrote the past, but because you finally reclaimed your presence from it. You stopped rehearsing the version of yourself that had to survive and chose to install the one that is ready to lead.

This is what it means to become energetically sovereign. Your energy is no longer owned by outdated experiences. Your attention is no longer hijacked by old codes. You become available to the now, fully. And the now is the only place real influence can exist.

When you stop living inside memory loops, your perception sharpens. You begin to notice what's really happening rather than filtering it through fear, shame, or regret. You can connect without the need for defense. You can speak without rehearsing safety. You can think without dragging the weight of outdated scripts into every decision.

This shift doesn't happen all at once. But every time you reclaim a piece of your energy, you gain more clarity, more space, more momentum. Eventually, the volume of the past fades. It no longer shouts over your intuition. And you realize something powerful: nothing back there has the right to define what you build next.

That's the moment the loop breaks. Not because you finally healed every scar, but because you stopped giving your future to a story that already ended.

Part IV. The Reality Rewrite

By the time you arrive here, something has already shifted. You're not reading these words the same way you would have at the beginning. You've peeled back layers. Questioned assumptions. Exposed internal code that once operated without your awareness. You've seen how your identity was not something fixed, but a system — programmable, responsive, influenceable.

Now comes the phase that most people never reach: the actual rewrite.

Many books and systems stop just before this moment. They inspire insight but leave you standing at the edge of change without a bridge to cross. That's not what this part is. This is where the shift becomes real. Not as theory. Not as an idea. But as reinstalled code that rewires your interaction with the external world.

You're no longer working only on yourself. You're working on the projection of reality that flows *from* yourself.

Reality is not a static field you're trapped in. It is a responsive interface. It reflects back not only your actions, but your signal. It responds to the authority you claim, the frame you hold, the meaning you assign. This final phase is about making that interface bend. Not by force. Not by effort. But by internal recalibration.

What you believe, you broadcast. What you embody, you receive confirmation of. But the twist most people miss is that these aren't affirmations or mind tricks. They're programs. You can write them. You can install them. And when they run, they produce results not because you're forcing life to comply, but because life *always* complies with your dominant code.

This section is not about becoming someone new. It's about aligning with the version of you that's always been possible but never permitted. It's about locking in new patterns until they are the default. Until they no longer feel like effort but inevitability.

You'll no longer be trying to manifest change. You'll *be* the change that shifts what reality mirrors back. And this is where real power lives: not in trying to convince reality to give you more, but in becoming the one it cannot help but respond to.

This is the rewrite. Not of the world outside you. But of the system you broadcast into it.

The rest will follow.

Chapter 9: Wire in Manifestation Triggers

Pattern Recognition as Power

You're not just reacting to life. You're decoding it. Whether you realize it or not, your brain is constantly scanning for patterns. It's trying to make sense of what's happening, what's predictable, and what's worth responding to. This isn't just a survival mechanism. It's your built-in tool for navigating and influencing reality. The problem is, most people use it unconsciously, letting old programs define what patterns are even *visible* to them.

Pattern recognition is the interface between what happens and what it *means*. But here's the key: it's not neutral. You don't see patterns objectively. You see them through the lens of your internal code. And that lens has been shaped by the past — by trauma, repetition, and social conditioning. That's why two people can live through the same event and take away completely different meanings. One sees an opportunity. The other sees a threat. Same data, different decoding system.

When your identity is still wired to the old framework, your brain filters reality in a way that reinforces what you already believe. You notice what confirms your limitations. You overlook what contradicts them. You mistake possibility for risk. You mistake feedback for failure. And all of that happens below the level of conscious thought.

This is why people stay stuck. Not because they lack intelligence, resources, or desire. But because they are blind to the patterns that would set them free. Or worse, they see them, but interpret them through a corrupted lens. The truth is, reality is full of repeating loops, mirrored signs, and fractal intelligence. It's not chaotic. It's coded. And when you begin to decode it accurately, it feels like everything starts talking to you. Not metaphorically. Literally. Conversations. Glitches. Coincidences. Delays. Sudden shifts. They all begin to mean something different — not because the world changed, but because *you* did.

There is a quiet confidence that arises when you start to recognize these patterns for what they really are. You stop trying to control everything directly. You stop wasting energy on outcomes. Instead, you tune into the signals that tell you where the code is pointing. You follow the movement, not the noise.

This shift does something powerful to your perception. You begin to see that what you once labeled as resistance was often redirection. That the thing you thought was failure was a correction of trajectory. That the person who triggered you wasn't your enemy, but a mirror of an internal file that needed updating. Suddenly, life isn't random anymore. It's readable. And once it's readable, it's influenceable.

But here's where the real upgrade happens: pattern recognition becomes a tool not just for *observing* reality, but for *steering* it. You don't just notice loops — you learn to end them. You don't just decode feedback — you use it to refine your internal alignment. You realize that power isn't in brute effort. It's in signal clarity. And the clearer your signal, the faster the feedback.

This is where many get overwhelmed. The deeper you go into this, the more patterns you begin to see — not just around you, but *in* you. Your emotional reactions. Your thought spirals. Your triggers. Your avoidance. All patterns. Not personal flaws. Not fixed traits. Just scripts that can be rewritten. But only if you can see them clearly.

That's where we go next.

When you bring awareness to a pattern, you collapse its unconscious grip. What once ran automatically now becomes a choice. That's the beginning of mastery. But awareness alone is not enough. You must go further into the structure of the pattern — understand what triggers it, what sustains it, and what identity it protects. Most patterns are not random behaviors. They are defense mechanisms, often disguised as preferences or personality traits. You repeat them not because they serve you, but because they once made you feel safe.

This is why pattern recognition must be coupled with internal stillness. Without that inner silence, you react to what you see instead of understanding it. Your mind jumps to fix or label the pattern, instead of letting it show you what it's made of. You override it too early or reinforce it without realizing. The true skill is learning to *observe* a pattern without feeding it. That's how it loses power. That's how you reclaim yours.

There's also a deeper layer. Patterns aren't just behavioral. They are energetic. You don't just act out loops. You emit them. People feel them before you speak. Rooms respond to them before you move. This is why two people can say the same words and get different results. The signal behind the words is different. One transmits clarity. The other transmits distortion. Reality doesn't respond to what you *intend*. It responds to what you *broadcast*.

Once you recognize that, your attention naturally shifts inward. You stop trying to change what's happening outside and start tracing the pattern at its root. You start asking different questions: What signal am I sending right now? What does this loop protect? Who do I think I need to be in order to stay safe? The answers to those questions often dismantle the pattern faster than any strategy could.

This also explains why certain lessons keep repeating in slightly different forms. New people. New environments. But the same emotional tone. Life is trying to show you something. Not to punish you, but to give you the chance to see clearly enough to choose differently. The moment you fully see the loop for what it is, and you stop reacting from the same identity, the pattern dissolves. Not because you fought it, but because you no longer *matched* it.

You become someone else. Someone who doesn't need the loop. Someone whose nervous system is no longer calibrated to that frequency. And because of that, your external world shifts with precision. Opportunities feel more aligned. People feel more real. Time feels more generous. Not by luck, but by coherence.

This is the core of pattern mastery. Not control. Not force. Clarity. When you can see a pattern without judging it, without collapsing into it, and without needing to fix it from fear, you begin to stand in a different power. You become someone who is no longer shaped by the past, but who shapes reality through presence.

That's where transformation accelerates. Because once you can do this with your thoughts and behaviors, you begin doing it with the world around you. You see the game. You understand the rhythm behind the noise. And you play from a position of awareness that most people never reach.

Pattern recognition becomes vision. And that vision becomes influence.

Thought > Emotion > Signal > Outcome

There's a hidden architecture behind every result you experience. It's not random, and it's not just about what you do. Every action you take, every reaction you offer, every "result" you call good or bad — they all stem from an invisible sequence: **Thought leads to Emotion, Emotion shapes Signal, Signal produces Outcome.**

Most people try to change outcomes by forcing behavior. They jump straight to action. They grind, overcompensate, overanalyze, and when the results don't change, they double down or spiral into frustration. The issue isn't that they're not trying hard enough. It's that they're intervening too far downstream. The real shift doesn't happen by pushing harder. It happens when you change the input.

Your dominant thoughts trigger an emotional climate. Not just fleeting feelings, but sustained internal atmospheres that become your emotional default. If you think in loops of fear, you feel uncertain. If you rehearse images of failure, you generate anxiety. And if your thoughts spiral around what might go wrong, you start embodying the vibration of avoidance, even when you smile on the surface.

That emotional climate is what begins to shape your **signal** — the invisible language you transmit at all times. This signal is not just metaphorical. It's a measurable field. It influences how people respond to you, how sensitive your nervous system becomes to patterns, and how your reality seems to "echo" your mood. You've seen this before. On days when you feel deeply grounded, clear, and decisive, the world seems to sync up. Conversations open more easily. Decisions come faster. Resistance feels minimal. It's not coincidence. It's coherence.

The signal is your transmission. It's not what you say, but what your system radiates. It comes from the integration of your thoughts and emotions. That integration creates a frequency, and that frequency shapes your reality. You attract not what you want, but what you are energetically aligned with. And alignment isn't about repeating affirmations. It's about shifting the sequence from the top.

When people feel stuck, what they're often experiencing is a signal mismatch. Their thoughts say, "I want abundance," but their emotional baseline is scarcity. Their actions are motivated by proving themselves, but underneath is a belief that they're not enough. This creates an incoherent signal — one that cancels itself out. The universe doesn't punish incoherence. It just reflects it. That reflection often shows up as mixed results, stop-start momentum, or emotional burnout.

To shift this, you need to slow the process down enough to witness it in motion. Begin at the source. What is the root thought pattern running right now? Is it grounded in truth, or is it a protective distortion? That one inquiry can interrupt the entire chain reaction before it cascades.

From there, you track the emotion it creates. Not just the emotion you name, but the one your body shows. Tension in the chest. Shallow breath. Disconnection. These are signals themselves. They tell you that the internal alignment is off. The body doesn't lie.

This is where most people stop — they become aware of the thoughts and feel the emotions, but they don't shift the signal. They intellectualize the pattern instead of reprogramming the source frequency.

To begin shifting that signal in real time, you must train your system to interrupt the emotional signal at the somatic level. That means not only identifying what emotion is present, but also changing the body's association to it in real time. If fear collapses the chest, open it. If anxiety tightens your gut, breathe deeper into your stomach. These subtle physical shifts start to rewire the internal map, because the body anchors your emotional patterns more than your conscious awareness does. When you shift your physical posture, you begin reversing the emotion it used to trigger.

From there, you embed a new signal through repetition and conscious direction. This doesn't mean forcing fake positivity. It means crafting an emotional resonance that's true, elevated, and sustainable. A thought like "I am becoming more stable every day" is far more effective than "I am already wealthy and powerful" if your system doesn't believe it yet. Truth is the carrier wave of energy. A false signal doesn't transmit cleanly. A believable, grounded affirmation that still lifts your state creates real alignment.

As you integrate the new emotional tone, the signal changes naturally. Your presence becomes less reactive. Your decisions start to reflect clarity instead of compulsion. People around you feel it even if they don't know why. That's because your signal has shifted at the core — and now the world is picking up on it.

What follows next is the unfolding of outcomes. The reality that once seemed resistant starts to respond differently. Conversations open. Serendipity increases. Opportunities you once felt shut out from start to orbit closer. You don't have to chase them. You've become compatible with them.

The trap for many is to interpret this as magical thinking, to assume the signal is just another metaphysical shortcut. But the real power comes from understanding it as a behavioral blueprint. When your signal is coherent, your actions become magnetic, your communication becomes more precise, and your intuition becomes sharper. You don't just feel better — you act better, choose better, and experience better.

This is not something you practice once and then forget. It's a living loop. Thoughts are constant, emotions shift, signals broadcast, outcomes reflect. The game is not to control every thought, but to know which ones matter. The goal isn't to feel perfect all the time, but to be aware of what your emotional baseline is signaling to the world.

One of the most underestimated tools is observation without reaction. The moment you can see a thought without becoming it, you've created enough distance to prevent it from becoming emotion. When you can feel an emotion without acting from it, you've stabilized your signal. And when your signal remains steady, even while life fluctuates, your outcomes begin to take on a new shape — not because you forced them, but because you stopped interfering with their alignment.

This is the core of internal congruence. The reality you experience is just the feedback loop of your internal signal. It will always find a way to mirror your inner structure. When you own that, you stop trying to control the mirror and start editing the source.

You are not just the thinker. You are the tuner. Your thoughts set the tone, your emotions amplify it, your signal sends it out, and the world responds accordingly. That is the sequence. That is the system. And now that you can see it, you are no longer inside the loop by default — you are the one programming it.

Embedding Manifestation Triggers Into Daily Life

Manifestation, when done consciously, isn't a once-a-day practice. It's not something you switch on for five minutes in the morning and then forget as the noise of the world takes over. The people who seem to live in alignment with their desires, who appear to draw opportunity into their orbit without force, aren't doing more. They've simply built internal mechanisms that keep their signal alive throughout the day.

This is the hidden layer most people miss: repetition isn't just about practice, it's about placement. If your highest state is locked inside your journal and never makes it to your kitchen, commute, or conversation, the signal doesn't hold. The key is embedding micro-triggers into your environment that remind your system of who you're becoming and what reality you're aligning to.

Think of your nervous system as a pattern-recognition machine. It's constantly scanning for cues that confirm or contradict your internal identity. If your space is neutral or worse, filled with symbols that echo your past struggles, your body will naturally anchor into a frequency that matches that state. So you don't just need a vision — you need cues. Visual, auditory, sensory, and spatial anchors that pull your consciousness back to alignment without needing to consciously effort every moment.

This doesn't mean plastering sticky notes all over your mirror with generic affirmations. That usually backfires because it overwhelms the mind or becomes invisible through repetition. The deeper work is about intentional placement. You embed the trigger where the old pattern once ruled.

For example, if you used to collapse into self-doubt while brushing your teeth in the morning, that's where you implant a signal of power. It could be a shift in your posture, a recalibration breath, or a private mantra spoken into the mirror that your system begins to associate with clarity instead of confusion. You're not repeating empty words. You're rewiring the body to respond differently in a familiar space.

Movement is also a powerful anchor. Most people carry an unconscious walk. Shoulders rounded, breath shallow, pace reactive. This reinforces the internal narrative without a word being spoken. But if you consciously embed a specific movement — a pause before entering a room, a grounding breath before speaking, a deliberate moment of presence before touching your phone — you begin to build new neurological bridges. These small acts create massive compounding effects because they shape how your body responds to the world, and how the world reads you in return.

Even objects can become manifestation anchors. Your phone wallpaper. The first sound you hear when you wake up. A piece of jewelry that isn't just aesthetic, but symbolic. These are not for show. They are private codes. They work not because they're magical, but because they carry emotional weight and intentional repetition. When you assign a new meaning to a neutral object and repeat that meaning enough, it becomes a trigger for the state you're calling in.

But none of this works if the system is overrun by noise. You cannot embed new patterns if your internal bandwidth is constantly hijacked. That's why a major part of embedding manifestation into your life isn't about adding more. It's about clearing interference. You begin to design your day in a way that reduces unnecessary cognitive load. When there is space in the system, a trigger can take root. When there is chaos, it gets drowned out.

And that brings us to one of the most important aspects of embedded manifestation: precision. It's not about being high vibe all the time or flooding your reality with vague positivity. It's about knowing which signal to amplify and where, so that the effect is both subtle and powerful.

You aren't trying to flood your environment with affirmation overload. You're weaving intention into the architecture of your day. The process is more about subtraction than addition. You remove cues that anchor you to lack, fatigue, or comparison. You disrupt default behaviors with subtle but intentional pattern breaks. And through repetition, those breaks become the new path of least resistance.

Your brain doesn't care if a pattern is empowering or limiting. It only cares if it's familiar. This is why change often feels unnatural at first. When you begin embedding new triggers, your system may resist. It's not because the trigger doesn't work. It's because the body is still loyal to the old sequence. That loyalty isn't emotional, it's neurological. You're rerouting electricity. And the only way to build the new circuit is by feeding it more current than the old one gets. That happens through volume and consistency.

So when you walk into your kitchen and place your hand flat on the counter for a second before reaching for your coffee, you're not doing something small. You're inserting a pause into a formerly unconscious loop. That pause creates space. And in that space, a new version of you can speak.

If your default mode is reaction, your triggers must slow the system down. If your default is indecision, your triggers must anchor certainty. If your default is self-censorship, your triggers must invite boldness. It's not one-size-fits-all. You don't embed someone else's rituals. You create ones that your nervous system will recognize as both safe and expansive.

This requires brutal honesty. You must know your own pressure points. The places where your energy collapses. The hours of the day when you betray your intention. The conversations where you shrink. These are not flaws. They are access points. You embed the trigger where the fracture lives.

Even your breath can become a signal. Most people breathe in ways that match their stress patterns without realizing it. Shallow breathing, tight jaw, constricted chest. If you train your body to associate a specific breath rhythm with a chosen state — grounded confidence, clarity, magnetism — you now carry a portable switch. It's not about deep breathing in general. It's about precision. One inhale, one exhale, embedded with meaning, executed in a moment where the past would have taken over.

These embedded signals are not tricks. They are technologies. You are engineering your reality through the body, not around it. And this is where so many people get stuck in the manifestation world. They keep trying to think their way into a new experience while dragging a nervous system calibrated for scarcity, for vigilance, for self-protection. Until the body is enrolled, the future cannot land.

What you're doing here is not cosmetic. You're changing your reflexes. You're altering the energetic code that governs how you move, how you speak, how you interpret reality. This is manifestation at its most granular level. Not as fantasy or abstract intention, but as embodied signal management.

Eventually, you won't need to remember the trigger. It will become part of your structure. You'll walk differently, speak differently, respond differently without trying to. That's the point. When the signal is internalized, reality shifts in response not because you're forcing it, but because you've become the version of yourself who lives there.

There's nothing accidental about the people who seem to attract what they want while others push and hustle and stay stuck. They've turned their life into a feedback loop that confirms their identity in motion. That loop is made of small moments, hidden cues, repeated decisions, and embedded signals that speak louder than effort ever could.

This is how you install manifestation into the code of your day. Quietly. Precisely. And permanently.

Chapter 10: Build the Perception Engine

Reality Is Input + Bias

Reality is not a fixed experience. It is filtered. You never interact with raw reality. You interact with **your version** of it, constructed by the data your brain receives and the biases that interpret that data. Two people can look at the same situation and live entirely different experiences, not because the situation changes, but because their filters do.

Your nervous system doesn't record objective truth. It records *what it thinks matters*. It takes in sensory input — sight, sound, language, movement — and passes it through your subconscious biases. What survives that filtration becomes your perception. What doesn't, gets discarded. And most of this happens without your awareness.

If you believe people are untrustworthy, your mind scans for evidence to support that. Not because you want it to. Because your brain is efficient. It learns what you value, even unconsciously, and then highlights it. This is known as selective attention. And it's not just about what you notice — it's about what your brain decides *you should notice*.

Now layer on confirmation bias. Once a belief is installed, the brain starts filtering out any data that contradicts it. If you've ever thought someone didn't like you and then saw every small gesture as proof, that wasn't your intuition speaking. That was bias, sharpening your focus on cues that matched your expectation. You weren't reading them. You were reading *your belief about them*.

This is the silent architecture behind so many limitations. People don't live small lives because their potential is small. They live small lives because their input and bias keep them trapped in a reality loop that reinforces itself. If all you're receiving is filtered through a belief system designed for survival, scarcity, or past pain, your nervous system cannot register expansion as safe. It reads it as a threat.

This is why you can do all the journaling, vision boards, and affirmations in the world, and still feel like you're stuck in the same emotional orbit. If the input stays the same — what you see, hear, consume, say, and think — and the bias remains unchallenged, then the output, your reality, doesn't shift.

But this also means power. Because it's not just that reality is filtered — it's that you can *consciously alter* the filters. You can feed your system new input and interrogate your existing bias until the lens changes. And when the lens changes, so does the world.

Let's go deeper. Your bias isn't just shaped by your thoughts. It's shaped by your *state*. If you're exhausted, hungry, emotionally overwhelmed, your brain will default to safety and caution. Your bias will tilt negative. Your perception will become defensive. The same opportunity that felt exciting yesterday now feels risky today. Nothing external changed. But your state did. Which means the same input is now interpreted differently.

This is how people unknowingly sabotage their own expansion. They assume their perception is neutral. They don't realize it's moving target. And if they don't regulate their state, their bias keeps reverting to an older, outdated map.

To break this loop, you have to become aware not just of what you think, but of how your *system* is interpreting what you see. You have to start noticing what data gets your attention, what stories you default to, and what assumptions fill in the gaps. Most bias lives in those gaps — the places where you don't have full information, so your mind invents it based on the past.

This is the starting point. Once you see the equation — input plus bias equals perceived reality — you no longer take your reactions or assumptions as truth. You begin to question the lens. You start to interrupt the loop. You become the architect of your perception.

One of the most powerful shifts you can make is to stop reacting to your perception as if it were fact. When you pause and recognize that your system is serving you a curated version of the world — one based on historical preference, emotional residue, and internalized beliefs — you gain the ability to step back and ask a better question: *What else could this mean?*

That question interrupts the automation. It slows the cognitive reflex just long enough for you to install choice. And that moment of choice is the key to rewriting reality. Because if perception is constructed, then it can be reconstructed. The same situation that felt like rejection can become redirection. The same silence that triggered fear can be interpreted as peace. The same challenge that stirred anxiety can be recast as initiation.

But that doesn't happen by thinking your way into a new lens. It happens by experiencing the world differently, again and again, until your system learns to expect something new. You have to prime it with upgraded input. You have to train it to notice different things. If your attention has been obsessively scanning for danger, it won't automatically look for opportunity. You must teach it.

This is not about fake positivity. It's not about ignoring danger or pretending everything is fine. It's about neutralizing the hijack that occurs when outdated bias decides the meaning of your life in real time. It's about reclaiming the authority to choose how you see.

When you do this work consistently, your nervous system begins to respond differently. You stop overreacting to old signals. You stop freezing at imagined threats. You start noticing opportunities that used to fly beneath your radar. Because the radar itself has changed. Your system no longer flags growth as a red alert. It starts to interpret progress as safety.

This internal safety is crucial. Without it, any attempt to reprogram your mindset is short-lived. You can visualize the future, recite affirmations, and set goals, but if your body still flinches at success or doubts pleasure, your bias will tilt you back toward the familiar. Not because it's right, but because it's known.

So part of the shift is nervous system conditioning. This means creating regulated states where your brain and body are no longer expecting chaos or rejection as the default. It also means gradually exposing yourself to new inputs — environments, people, conversations, stimuli — that represent the world you want to live in. If you've only ever been around scarcity, then wealth will feel threatening until it becomes familiar. If you've only seen love through the lens of control, then freedom may seem empty until your system relearns connection.

Bias isn't moral. It's mechanical. It will keep serving you the same version of reality until you intervene. But once you understand the formula — once you really internalize that what you perceive is not the world but your filter — then every interaction becomes a mirror. Every trigger becomes a diagnostic. Every assumption becomes a doorway. You stop playing defense. You start designing your experience.

This is not instant. But it is permanent. You don't have to escape your old patterns. You have to outgrow them. And that happens by consistently feeding your mind new data, while simultaneously regulating your internal state so that your bias no longer interprets expansion as danger. It is in this deliberate balance — of awareness, input, and nervous system coherence — that perception recalibrates.

Reality responds to the lens through which it is viewed. Change the lens, and the world shows up differently. You're not here to chase external validation for your perception. You're here to refine the instrument that shapes it. Because once your system learns how to process the same input through a more empowered bias, reality doesn't just appear different. It *becomes* different. And so do you.

How to Control What the Brain Sees and Ignores

Your brain is not designed to show you the truth. It's designed to show you what is *useful for your survival*, based on what you already believe, expect, or fear. It is not objective. It is predictive. And that simple fact explains why two people can live through the exact same experience and walk away with completely different interpretations. One saw opportunity. The other saw threat. The event wasn't the difference. The filter was.

This filter is known as the **Reticular Activating System** (RAS), and it functions like a mental gatekeeper. It determines what information gets passed to your conscious mind and what gets discarded. Every second, your senses take in millions of bits of data. But your brain can only consciously process a fraction of that. So it makes a decision — moment by moment — about what deserves your attention.

That decision is not random. The RAS is trained over time. If you've spent years expecting to be rejected, it will highlight moments that seem to confirm that fear, even when the full picture says otherwise. If you believe success is for other people, not you, your brain will ignore signals that prove you're actually progressing. It will magnify evidence that keeps your identity intact. This isn't a flaw. It's an efficiency mechanism. But it can lock you into a psychological loop where the brain is filtering reality in ways that preserve limitation.

The result? You literally don't see what contradicts your script. You could walk past the solution to your biggest problem and not recognize it. You could meet someone who genuinely sees your potential and brush them off. You could have a moment of freedom and immediately tense up, because your system tags it as unfamiliar, and therefore unsafe.

This is why surface-level change rarely lasts. You can try to "think positive," but if your RAS is still coded to filter out abundance, your brain won't even register it. You'll stay locked in patterns, not because you lack willpower, but because your internal filter is making decisions before your conscious mind even gets involved.

To regain control, you must train the filter.

This begins with conscious intent, but it must go deeper than affirmations or motivation. The brain needs repetition, emotional charge, and context. You have to consistently feed your system signals that reflect the reality you want to internalize — not just once, but daily, until the unfamiliar becomes familiar and the bias shifts.

For example, if you want to rewire your brain to notice opportunity instead of threat, you must practice recognizing even the smallest signs of progress or safety. You must pause when something goes right and *feel it fully*, letting the body memorize the sensation. Because your nervous system is watching too. It's not just what you think — it's what you *experience*.

This process takes intention. But once you understand how to work with your RAS instead of against it, you're no longer at the mercy of unconscious filters. You can walk into the same environment, with the same people, and notice a completely different layer of reality. Not because the world changed. Because *your access to it changed.*

Your entire experience of life is shaped by what your brain allows in. You're not trying to force the world to be different. You're teaching your mind to stop ignoring the parts that are already aligned with where you're going. And once that shift locks in, reality starts to reflect back a completely different set of possibilities.

The more emotionally neutral your nervous system becomes in the presence of unfamiliar signals, the more open your perception becomes. Safety creates space. When your body no longer treats growth or change as a threat, your filter begins to relax. And that's when you start noticing what's always been available but previously dismissed or overlooked.

This is why nervous system regulation isn't just a healing tool, but a strategy for clarity. If your baseline is anxiety, your perception will skew toward spotting problems before possibilities. The RAS assumes that anything not marked as dangerous is irrelevant, and that bias makes sure you keep seeing the same version of life. But once you train your system to remain calm in the unknown, the signal starts to shift. Calm becomes a permission slip. Curiosity returns. Pattern recognition expands.

That's the pivot point. From that place, your brain begins to show you the world differently. You may catch a facial expression you'd normally ignore. You may read between the lines of a conversation. You might hear yourself speak a sentence and suddenly realize it doesn't align with who you are anymore. These micro-adjustments are signs that your filter is opening. Your awareness is no longer locked into only what confirms the past.

To make this sustainable, the practice must move beyond theory. It requires you to intervene gently in the moments your brain defaults to the familiar. This happens most often in reaction. When something frustrates you, confuses you, or triggers insecurity, the filter contracts. But that is also the window of influence. If you can pause and redirect the signal — not by suppressing it, but by re-choosing your focus — you begin teaching your system to upgrade the lens.

That upgrade doesn't come from force. It comes from repetition with precision. It's not enough to repeat new beliefs passively. You must *embody* them with full sensory presence. That means noticing when you feel what you want to feel and anchoring it. It also means noticing when your system tries to reject a new possibility and staying in the room long enough for it to lose its threat charge.

The RAS is programmable. But it is stubborn. It listens to frequency and frequency only. What do you talk about most? What do you rehearse emotionally? What do you label as "normal" even when it doesn't serve you? These signals train the filter. If you say you want change but continue to speak the language of lack, your filter will continue to scan for confirmation of lack. And it will always find it.

Clarity is not just about intelligence. It's about access. The sharpest mind in the world is still subject to distortion if the filter hasn't been reprogrammed. This is why growth often begins with subtraction. Not by adding more goals, but by removing noise. Not by chasing more information, but by getting quiet enough to hear what the brain was already muting.

The question is not just "what do I want to see?" but "what have I trained myself to ignore?" That question cuts through self-deception. It confronts you with the cost of your current lens. And it opens the door to a far more powerful one — a lens that sees not only what is, but what is possible.

Control over perception is control over direction. When you train your brain to stop filtering out power, synchronicity accelerates. You begin noticing patterns that feel too aligned to be accidental. They're not. They were just invisible before. Because you hadn't yet become someone who could see them.

That's the difference between reacting to life and shaping it. One is unconscious input. The other is trained attention. What you see determines what you do. What you do determines who you become. And who you become determines what your mind believes is possible to see. Loop closed. Signal upgraded. Reality transformed.

The Reticular Activation Ritual

The Reticular Activating System (RAS) is not a metaphor. It's a real structure in your brainstem that acts as a filter between your sensory input and conscious awareness. But what most people don't realize is how programmable this filter really is. You don't just passively experience the world through your RAS. You train it—moment by moment—through focus, repetition, and emotion.

If you've ever decided to buy a specific car and then suddenly started seeing that exact model everywhere, that wasn't a coincidence. Your brain didn't change the world. It changed what it allowed you to notice. This is the essence of the RAS at work: it selectively gates information to align with what it believes is relevant to you. The catch? It doesn't care if that relevance is empowering or limiting. It simply follows instructions.

And most people are giving it the wrong ones.

Without conscious input, the RAS learns from repetition. It gives priority to what you rehearse, even if what you rehearse is anxiety, self-doubt, or fear. If you constantly entertain the thought that you're unlucky or invisible or behind in life, the RAS will ensure you see more evidence to support it. This is not just mindset. It's mechanics. Your filter tightens around those beliefs, suppressing contradictory data, even if it's right in front of you.

Which brings us to the ritual.

This is not a routine. It's not a positive affirmation loop. The Reticular Activation Ritual is about commanding the filter—deliberately and consistently—so it bends toward expansion. Not just to help you feel good, but to open perceptual gates that were previously shut. When executed with precision, it doesn't just prime your focus. It rewires the type of information your brain allows in.

That distinction is everything. You're not trying to change reality by forcing it. You're shifting your relationship to it by recalibrating what your system perceives as signal vs noise. In this sense, the ritual is a form of neural editing. You're not waiting for reality to show you something new. You're teaching your perception to look differently at what's already present.

The ritual works by leveraging three core components: focus, embodiment, and emotional anchoring. Focus determines what gets through the filter. Embodiment translates that focus into sensation. And emotion locks the experience into your neural map. When all three are activated, the RAS updates its criteria. It begins treating your new focus as the reference point. But this only works if your nervous system believes the signal is safe. That's why the ritual must be practiced in a calm, regulated state—not in urgency, not in grasping, and not in self-correction. If you try to force the ritual to work from a place of desperation, your body will register contradiction. The result? No perceptual shift. Your RAS will tag the ritual as cognitive dissonance and revert to the old filter.

This is why so many people repeat affirmations and visualizations without results. The input isn't neutral. It's wrapped in resistance. And resistance doesn't program the RAS—it confuses it. The system doesn't respond to words. It responds to signal. And your true signal is the combination of thought, body, and feeling over time.

To begin this shift, you don't need to believe in magic. You only need to be precise. Your goal is not to flood your mind with fantasies. Your goal is to saturate your system with selective awareness. This is a technical adjustment in perception—not a motivational boost. And it must be treated with the same intentionality you'd bring to tuning an instrument. Subtle misalignment breaks the signal. Precision activates it.

Start by identifying a focus statement that reflects the version of reality you are ready to align with. This is not about forcing optimism or repeating vague affirmations. Your statement must be grounded, specific, and felt. It should be a clear directive to your system, not a wish or a hope. For example, instead of saying, "I am wealthy," a more powerful signal would be, "I notice evidence every day that my influence is expanding." The language here invites your RAS to search for signs, not to challenge belief.

Speak this statement aloud in a calm, clear tone. Don't rush. Let it hang in the air for a moment, then bring your attention to your body. Where do you feel openness or resistance? Don't try to fix it. Just notice. The body is the amplifier. Your job is not to override it but to tune it.

Now pair the statement with a moment of physical anchoring. This can be as subtle as placing your hand over your chest, adjusting your posture, or pressing your feet into the ground. The goal is to associate the thought with a consistent somatic cue. When repeated over time, this cue becomes a neural shortcut. Your system will eventually begin responding to the gesture itself by activating the desired filter, even without the words.

Next, bring in emotion. Not in a performative or exaggerated way, but as a deliberate choice. Ask yourself, "What would it feel like in my nervous system if this focus was already true?" Wait for the answer to arrive. Let it settle into your body as a real experience, even if just for a moment. This is not about fooling yourself. It's about introducing a new signal and allowing your system to register it as safe, accessible, and familiar.

When done correctly, you may notice a slight shift in attention. You may find yourself scanning the room differently, hearing things you would have ignored, or becoming more sensitive to alignment and misalignment. That's your RAS beginning to adapt. It's subtle, but it's real.

The ritual is most effective when practiced consistently, especially in transitional moments: right after waking, before stepping into a key environment, or when you notice your awareness shrinking. But it's not about volume. Ten seconds of precise, embodied activation is more powerful than ten minutes of disjointed repetition. Quality creates signal. Signal shapes filter. Filter guides perception.

Over time, your system will begin to anticipate the state rather than resist it. This is where the shift becomes effortless. The RAS, once trained, does not need constant supervision. It begins to reinforce its own programming. You'll start noticing people, opportunities, and feedback that support your selected frame, not because they weren't there before, but because you've finally permitted your awareness to register them.

This is the hidden architecture of transformation. It's not in what you do, but in what you begin to notice and respond to differently. Most people exhaust themselves trying to change external outcomes while their perceptual filter keeps selecting from the same narrow bandwidth. The Reticular Activation Ritual reverses that equation. It gives you access to new inputs, which create new responses, which generate new outcomes—without brute force.

You are not editing the external world. You are editing your access to it. That's the true leverage of this work. When you recalibrate what gets in, you recalibrate what becomes possible. The rest of the system follows. And once your nervous system treats expansion as familiar, the resistance fades. What once felt invisible becomes obvious. What once felt impossible becomes automatic. Not because you changed everything, but because you finally began to see.

Chapter 11: Master Internal State Control

Mood as a Command Line

Most people think of mood as something that happens to them. A byproduct of hormones, weather, or external events. It's treated as background noise, a passive state that rises and falls, barely acknowledged unless it interferes with performance. But mood is far more than atmosphere. It's command.

Every system in your body listens to mood like software listens to code. Mood delivers the tone that the rest of your biology, perception, and behavior follow. It determines what gets filtered in and what gets ignored. It biases decisions, shifts memory retrieval, alters how you perceive time, and even affects what you believe is possible.

Mood is not emotional chaos. It's structured input. And when you don't recognize that, you start unconsciously responding to a command line you didn't write.

Imagine two people entering the same room. One is in a low mood: unfocused, agitated, expectant of disappointment. The other carries a mood of quiet certainty. Even without saying a word, they notice different things. They interpret silences differently. They respond to cues in ways that either generate connection or push it away. One sees a closed door. The other sees an opening. This isn't about optimism. It's about the lens being installed through the operating system.

Your mood sets the parameters of how your nervous system functions. It either activates the parasympathetic state of flow and responsiveness or locks you into survival coding: vigilance, contraction, and reactive patterning. What's vital to understand here is that this isn't theoretical. It's physiological. Your immune system, your digestion, your cognitive access, and your muscle tension all shift based on your prevailing mood.

This is why, when you attempt to make strategic decisions from a low mood, things feel heavy or blurry. Your system has interpreted the low signal as a warning and begins stripping away your access to creative and future-oriented thought. You may notice that in low moods, you become past-oriented. You loop. You fixate. Your body subtly prepares for defense instead of expansion. And because you don't feel the shift as a loud alarm, you don't question it. You assume it's real.

Mood, in this way, becomes an invisible author. It rewrites how you view your own capabilities. It edits your sense of control. And once you believe that mood is fixed, you stop questioning the commands it's giving. You begin to obey them.

There is a way to break this loop, and it doesn't start with forcing a better mood. It starts with recognizing that mood is not just a response but a broadcast. And once you begin to sense it that way, you can choose not only whether to react to it, but whether to rewrite it at the source.

The nervous system responds more to signal than reason. It listens for tone, for rhythm, for coherence. It responds to felt safety, not verbal reassurance. So the key isn't to talk yourself into a better mood. It's to input a new signal—one that your system can believe and align with.

This is where subtle practices become powerful. Not because they are dramatic, but because they bypass the logical filters and reach the command line directly.

The system is always scanning for congruence. If your internal state doesn't match the cues it receives through breath, posture, voice, and environment, it stays in a kind of static. This is why simply thinking positive thoughts or repeating affirmations in a tense or anxious body rarely works. The command line doesn't respond to words alone. It listens to frequency. Input needs to feel real, believable, grounded in sensory coherence.

You can influence this system through micro-signals. Breath is one of the most powerful tools. Not because of what it represents symbolically, but because of what it does neurologically. A slow, deep exhale that activates the vagus nerve tells the nervous system, "You're safe. Stand down." That signal is more powerful than any mental override. In that moment, your biology receives a new directive. Your chemistry begins to shift, attention reorganizes, and your sense of self adjusts accordingly.

Movement is another input channel. Not forced exertion, but intentional rhythm. A walk with full sensory presence. The way you carry your spine. The openness of your chest. Each of these signals changes what the system believes to be true. That truth isn't conceptual. It is built from repeated evidence the body can feel.

There's also the role of language, not as surface chatter, but as an anchor. The words you use internally sculpt how your system orients. A phrase like "nothing works for me" runs like a background command. It infects the logic tree of your day. Without being questioned, it informs how your system interprets obstacles, social cues, even silence. On the other hand, a phrase like "I can navigate this" does not pretend certainty. It simply tells the system to remain open. That openness is where capacity lives.

Mood hijacks happen most often when we lose that gap between internal dialogue and the physical signal. You feel a dip in energy, and the mind rushes in to make meaning out of it: "I'm off. I'm unmotivated. I can't focus." The label becomes its own loop. Soon, it is not just a mood but a conclusion about your capability. But if you can catch that moment—if you can question the speed with which meaning is assigned—you disrupt the loop. You reclaim authorship.

It's not about pretending to be in a better mood. It's about updating the source code by influencing the inputs. You cannot always choose the thoughts that arise, but you can decide how much weight you give them. You can slow the breath. You can relax the jaw. You can sit or stand in a way that says, "This body is not in crisis." And by doing so, you interrupt the old command line. You stop reinforcing outdated scripts.

This isn't a trick. It's neural training. And the more often you do it, the more easily your system defaults to a baseline of responsiveness rather than reaction. You start to experience yourself not as a mood, but as the one who sets the tone. This distinction is everything. Once you stop confusing your state with your identity, you stop obeying every signal as if it were truth. You start asking better questions, making clearer decisions, and filtering experience through a lens that serves your direction instead of derailing it.

Mood is not background noise. It is the interface through which you experience reality. When you claim it, you change the system. You shift from running old programs into writing new ones. Not by force, but by precision. Not by pressure, but by presence. Mood is a command line. The question is: who's typing?

State Stacking: Layering Emotional Power

Your nervous system doesn't operate in isolation. It builds momentum. Every emotion you experience leaves behind a residue that either sharpens or distorts your next response. What most people think of as a random mood swing is often just the consequence of unconscious state stacking, where one emotional imprint bleeds into the next without interruption or awareness.

State stacking happens automatically, but it can also be done deliberately. When you understand how to guide it, you shift from being at the mercy of emotional momentum to becoming the architect of it. This shift is not about suppression or control. It's about intentional layering—building a sequence of emotional states that reinforce clarity, power, and direction.

Think of each emotional state as a frequency you can tune into. When you feel calm, focused, or assertive, that isn't just an inner experience. It becomes a field that your entire nervous system organizes around. And that field influences how you perceive reality, how others respond to you, and what possibilities appear in your awareness. One state opens a doorway. Another one shuts it. What you're stacking is access.

You might start with something simple, like grounding. That could be as subtle as a change in breathing or body awareness. Once that base layer is active, you add something like gratitude. But not as a forced mental exercise—gratitude as a visceral state. You recall a specific moment that generates the feeling, not just the thought. Then you layer confidence, perhaps through a memory of something you once mastered, even if small. Each layer adds weight, shape, and complexity to the emotional structure you're building internally.

This is not a formula. It's a skill. And like any skill, it improves through repetition, nuance, and feedback from your own body. The key is not to rush the layering. You don't move on from one state until it becomes real enough to feel in your breath, your posture, your voice. Otherwise, you're stacking thoughts, not states—and that won't shift your nervous system or your field of influence.

When done properly, state stacking creates an internal architecture that is much harder to shake. You no longer enter situations from a neutral or reactive baseline. You enter already layered with inner resources. This is what gives certain people their unmistakable presence. It's not charisma. It's not magic. It's inner sequencing. You're not just showing up—you're arriving with an energetic echo behind you. That echo is the sum of the states you've layered before you even walk into the room.

This practice also creates resilience. When you're layered with intention, you're less likely to collapse into old patterns. Even if a trigger or challenge appears, it lands on top of a reinforced system. Instead of spiraling, you respond from the version of you that has already chosen alignment. You're not pulled back into the oldest version of yourself. You hold your frame, because you've built it in advance.

There's a deeper benefit too: identity begins to shift. As you repeatedly stack powerful emotional states, your nervous system updates its baseline expectations. The old, familiar moods that once defined your sense of self begin to lose their hold. You stop identifying with contraction. You begin to associate your center with openness, clarity, strength. This rewires your perception of what's normal for you, not just in mood, but in life quality.

To stack effectively, you must learn to pause between layers. This is not a rush to reach a peak state, but a deliberate process of integration. You're not just collecting emotions. You're giving each one time to settle into your physiology. It's a kind of emotional craftsmanship—waiting just long enough for a state to become embodied before laying the next one over it.

The first few times, it will feel subtle. You might wonder if anything is really changing. But that's only because you're used to being flooded by reactive states that scream for attention. Intentional states don't always arrive with drama. They arrive with stability. You'll know it's working when your reactions become slower, your awareness more spacious, and your body starts responding differently to situations that used to hijack you.

Once you've learned to feel the transition between layers, you can begin to sequence states based on the outcomes you want to amplify. If you're preparing for deep focus, you might layer stillness with curiosity, then follow with clarity. If you're moving into leadership or influence, you might stack grounding with personal power, followed by compassion. Each combination alters how your system broadcasts. It changes your field, your perception, and the response you elicit from the world around you.

What makes this so powerful is that it bypasses willpower. You're not forcing yourself to behave differently. You're creating the internal conditions that make new behaviors natural. That is the real secret to change. People stay stuck not because they lack discipline, but because their emotional architecture is still wired for the old identity. State stacking rewires that architecture from the inside.

Eventually, this becomes less of a ritual and more of a baseline. You begin to wake up with a sense of agency over how you will move through the day. Instead of defaulting to external cues, you make internal choices. You shift from reacting to shaping. And that shift compounds. The longer you live this way, the more automatic it becomes. You no longer have to remind yourself who you are becoming. You feel it, layer by layer, every morning, in your body.

There is a moment in this practice where you'll notice that your external world begins to adjust. People start responding to you differently, even though you haven't said much. Opportunities arise without force. Conversations open without pushing. This is not magic. It's attunement. When your internal state is aligned and stable, it becomes a quiet instruction to your environment. It's not about commanding others. It's about making coherence so palpable within you that it becomes impossible to ignore.

One of the most transformative uses of state stacking is to exit a spiral. In those moments when your nervous system is pulled into fear, irritation, or doubt, you now have a sequence to return to. You don't need to solve the trigger. You don't need to win the argument in your head. You only need to choose a different state and begin the layering process again. One breath, one memory, one shift at a time.

What you're doing is building a library of internal access points. Each emotional state becomes a tool. And once you've practiced them enough, you can activate them almost instantly. The nervous system learns through pattern. It doesn't care about motivation. It cares about repetition. What you practice, you become. What you layer, you embody. What you embody, you radiate.

That is emotional power. Not loud, not performative, but felt. By you first, and then by everything you touch.

Overriding the Nervous System

The nervous system is your internal gatekeeper. It decides what feels safe, what feels possible, and what gets shut down before you even notice it. Long before the mind creates meaning, the body is already reacting. It's not thinking in words. It's scanning for patterns, checking for threat, interpreting signals at a speed faster than conscious thought. And most people are living their lives in response to that invisible scan.

This is why deep change cannot happen through mindset alone. You can repeat affirmations and visualize outcomes, but if your nervous system has been wired to associate that outcome with danger, it will quietly sabotage your progress. Not because it wants to hurt you, but because it thinks it is protecting you. It is loyal to what is familiar. Safety, to the nervous system, means predictability.

For many, the current version of "normal" is rooted in stress, low-level fear, or emotional shutdown. The nervous system has learned to equate those patterns with survival. This is especially true for people who have experienced chaos, criticism, or neglect in formative years. The body becomes trained to anticipate stress even in moments of peace. It waits for the next threat. It flinches inward. And in doing so, it blocks the signal of growth.

To override this, you have to speak in the language the nervous system understands. It does not respond to logic. It responds to rhythm, breath, posture, repetition, and sensory feedback. You cannot argue your way into a regulated state. You have to feel your way there, and that begins with noticing how your system reacts to potential expansion.

Most people think their fear of change is a flaw. But often it's a form of protection. The nervous system sees "change" as a possible destabilizer. Even success can feel threatening if the body has no reference point for what safety looks like at that level. This is why so many people get close to their breakthrough, then sabotage it without knowing why. The subconscious signal says, "We don't know what comes next. Retreat."

You override that pattern by increasing familiarity with the unfamiliar. This is not done through intensity but through repetition and pacing. If you can create even a small feeling of safety within a new action, the nervous system begins to recalibrate. It learns that this new input is not a threat. That success does not mean loss. That visibility does not mean attack. That peace does not mean vulnerability.

One of the simplest but most profound tools for this is to use micro exposure. You take the thing your system fears and introduce it in a manageable, low-stakes form. Not to force yourself through it, but to watch how your body reacts. Do your shoulders tighten? Does your breath become shallow? Do you feel the urge to distract yourself? These are not signs of failure. They are data. They reveal the places where your system still equates expansion with risk.

Once you've located that response, the next step is to regulate *within* the exposure, not after it. This is where real override begins. You stay present, slow your breath, lengthen your exhale, and anchor into the part of you that knows this moment is not dangerous. Not to fight the reaction, but to create a new imprint. The nervous system learns not through force, but through presence.

Over time, this process builds a new baseline. What once triggered contraction now holds the possibility for calm. What used to feel like a threat begins to register as safe. This is not a mindset shift alone. It's a physiological reprogramming. The nervous system, once conditioned to scan for danger, begins to orient toward possibility. This is what makes transformation sustainable. You are not forcing yourself into a new version of your life. You are becoming someone who can actually hold it without collapse.

The mistake many people make is trying to leap over the body's resistance with sheer willpower. They chase bigger goals, louder affirmations, and more intense strategies, thinking this will drown out the fear. But the nervous system does not respond to pressure. It responds to safety. If your internal state is flooded, no amount of external pressure will integrate the new identity. In fact, it creates more fragmentation. The external begins to grow, but the internal cannot support it. And eventually, something breaks. You do not have to fight your nervous system to move forward. You have to bring it with you. This means building a bridge between the self you are now and the self you are becoming, not by pretending the fear isn't real, but by creating safety within the fear. That is how integration happens. That is how momentum becomes embodiment.

It's also why emotional suppression doesn't work. You can't override the system by ignoring the signals. If anything, repression only strengthens the old circuits. It buries the energy deeper into the body, where it becomes tension, disassociation, chronic fatigue, or impulsive sabotage. The real override happens when you allow the signal to surface without obeying it. You let the fear rise, but you stay anchored. You let the sensation move through, but you choose your behavior consciously. That's what changes the wiring. You become a clear signal amidst the noise.

One of the clearest indicators that you are overriding your nervous system in a healthy way is your ability to stay open while uncomfortable. Can you remain relaxed in uncertainty? Can you feel your heart race without attaching a story to it? Can you notice the contraction and still move forward, slowly, intentionally, without collapsing into reaction or retreat?

This is not about becoming numb or fearless. It's about developing internal flexibility. The ability to be with your inner experience without becoming it. That space between stimulus and response is the seat of your power. It is where identity evolves. It is where your signal begins to override the default programming.

With practice, you'll notice that your baseline begins to rise. The situations that used to trigger shutdown become neutral. The ones that felt overwhelming become manageable. The places where your body used to signal "no" now begin to soften into "maybe," and eventually into "yes." This is nervous system override in real time. Subtle. Gradual. Irrevocable.

You are not just thinking differently. You are becoming someone different. Not through force, but through trust. Trust in your capacity to hold what you once avoided. Trust in your ability to stay in your body when it wants to leave. Trust in the intelligence of your system to adapt, recalibrate, and evolve.

That is how you override the nervous system. Not by dominating it, but by leading it. You become the one who sets the tone. Who signals safety in moments that used to collapse you. Who teaches the body, again and again, that this new life is not just possible, but safe to receive. And that, perhaps, is the most powerful signal of all.

Chapter 12: Lock the System

Loop Closure and Identity Stabilization

Change does not stick until the brain believes the loop is complete. You may take action, feel a shift, even experience success. But if the identity hasn't been stabilized through closure, the nervous system will look for ways to return to the familiar. The loop you started stays open, energetically and psychologically, until something signals, "This is safe now. This is who I am."

The mind is constantly seeking resolution. When it doesn't get it, it replays experiences like static. A decision not followed through. A conversation that ended without clarity. A goal achieved but not integrated. All of these leave loops open. And each open loop carries a tension. That tension pulls on your attention, fragments your energy, and leaves your new identity vulnerable to collapse.

Think of a loop like a neurological contract. You initiate a change and your subconscious begins watching. Is this real? Is this consistent? Is this safe? If the loop is closed with reinforcement and clarity, the subconscious accepts the upgrade. If it's left open, even after action has been taken, the system eventually defaults to its last known stable identity.

This is why people revert after breakthroughs. They believe the moment was enough. They felt different. They acted different. But the closure never happened. So the transformation remains an event, not a new foundation.

To close the loop, you must anchor the new identity not just in thought, but in perception and behavior. This is not about repetition for repetition's sake. It's about strategic confirmation. The mind needs to see, feel, and believe that what just happened is real and that it aligns with who you now are.

This is especially true when identity is shifting rapidly. If you're moving from someone who used to doubt, overthink, or self-sabotage, into someone who leads, influences, and takes space, the distance between the old self and the new one can feel unstable. You've made the leap, but the emotional infrastructure hasn't caught up yet.

This is where loop closure becomes critical. If you don't complete the signal, your system reads the gap as danger. Even if things are improving, the unfamiliarity itself feels unsafe. So the body tugs you back into the role it knows, the one with historical stability, regardless of how limiting it was.

But once a loop is closed with precision, the stabilization begins. The new version of you doesn't just visit the surface. It lands. It gets reinforced in how you speak, how you respond, how you see yourself in the mirror. The mind doesn't have to keep checking, "Is this real?" because it has evidence. The loop doesn't need to stay open because the cycle has completed.

This is not about perfection. It's about congruence. The way you think, act, and feel begins to align. And that alignment creates stability. From that point forward, you are not performing the new identity. You are operating from it. The energy of proving is replaced with the energy of knowing. There's nothing left to resolve.

To reach this point, though, the reinforcement must happen in a precise window. This is where most people hesitate or get distracted. They feel the change starting, but they don't mark it. They don't confirm it. They don't witness themselves fully as the new self. So the shift becomes a spark instead of a flame.

The window to close a loop is brief but powerful. The moment the shift occurs—emotionally, mentally, or behaviorally—you are standing at a threshold. If you reinforce the new reality right there, the subconscious starts accepting it as the new baseline. If not, the window narrows, and the mind begins scanning for inconsistencies. It asks, "Was this real, or was it just temporary?"

To reinforce the loop, you must consciously witness the shift. This means naming it to yourself, feeling it in the body, and anchoring it with deliberate action. For example, if you just made a different decision than your old self would have, pause and acknowledge it. Let yourself feel the significance. Reflect on how this choice reflects who you are becoming. This self-witnessing tells the nervous system, "This is not an anomaly. This is the new normal."

Then comes physical anchoring. Embodiment locks in identity. A small but deliberate ritual—a gesture, a sentence spoken aloud, a new way of moving—can register as a closing act. Think of it as sealing a letter before sending it. Without the seal, the message is incomplete. With it, the brain receives the signal: this part of the transformation is done. It's safe to move forward from here.

Another form of closure is reflection through story. How you talk about yourself—internally and externally—either reopens old loops or stabilizes new ones. When you frame a shift as final, you reduce the subconscious urge to loop back. Say to yourself, "That version of me is no longer active," or "This is how I do things now." These micro-declarations carry more weight than we realize. They shape the story your nervous system uses to define self.

Patterns that resist closure often stem from unprocessed identity conflict. If a part of you is still attached to who you were, it will sabotage the stabilization process. That part may fear being left behind, or worry about judgment, loss, or the discomfort of growth. Loop closure, then, also requires integration. Not rejecting the old self, but absorbing its lessons, releasing its role, and making peace with its expiration.

Closure doesn't mean pretending the past didn't happen. It means removing the energetic charge. When a loop is closed, the memory may remain, but the emotional tug disappears. You stop reacting from the wound or the habit. You act from present intention. Stabilization becomes possible because there is no more internal tug-of-war.

The final layer is repetition with awareness. Not mechanical repetition, but conscious reinforcement. Every time you choose the new identity in action, the brain locks in the signal more deeply. The system learns through consistency. It learns through evidence. And once that evidence accumulates, you don't have to fight to stay in the new state. It becomes who you are, not what you're trying to do.

Stabilization is not about over-control. It's about creating coherence. When your thoughts, emotions, and behaviors match the identity you've claimed, the system relaxes. It no longer questions or resists. You stop leaking energy into doubt, and instead begin channeling that energy into forward motion. Momentum builds. Belief becomes automatic. Reality responds accordingly. At this stage, transformation moves out of the realm of effort and into the realm of embodiment. You are no longer managing change. You are living it. The loop has closed, the identity is stabilized, and your nervous system now sees this version of you as the safest, most efficient operating system. That's when you stop bouncing between versions of yourself. That's when things click into place.

Habitual Integration: Rituals That Make It Stick

The difference between temporary change and permanent transformation is integration. It's not what you do once that reprograms your reality. It's what you do repeatedly, with intention, until your nervous system no longer sees it as new. Integration is not about discipline in the traditional sense. It's about embedding the new identity into your automatic systems—until it becomes the default.

Every belief, emotional state, and identity you've ever operated from was taught to your system through repetition. Not grand, singular events, but daily reinforcement. This is how trauma embeds. This is also how power embeds. The mind favors patterns. The nervous system favors familiarity. And the unconscious favors whatever it has seen most often—regardless of whether it's empowering or limiting.

So if you want your shifts to last, they need to be *coded into your day*. Not as another task, but as a woven thread. This is where ritual becomes essential. A ritual is not just a habit. It's a signal. It tells the subconscious: this moment matters. And when something matters, the mind listens. Repeated moments of meaningful attention are what wire new identity loops into place.

The most powerful rituals aren't always complex. They're intentional. They carry emotional charge. They map to identity. For example, you can anchor a future identity with a morning ritual that includes three components: a movement that wakes the body, a phrase that affirms the version of you you are becoming, and a visualization that evokes emotional embodiment. What matters is not the time spent but the clarity of signal sent.

Integration happens fastest when the new behaviors aren't isolated from the rest of your life. Instead, they become the *lens* through which your entire day is lived. If you only feel powerful when meditating, but disempowered at work, the nervous system won't register true change. Rituals that stick are those that *link states* across contexts. You rehearse confidence not just in stillness, but while walking, working, speaking, and deciding.

That's why one of the most underestimated forms of integration is micro-rehearsal. Throughout the day, without stopping your life, you can re-enter your chosen identity for ten seconds at a time. The version of you who already has what you want—how would they answer this message? How would they carry their body? How would they move through this store, this call, this meeting?

Each of these tiny moments is a vote cast in favor of the identity you are stabilizing. And with each vote, the old wiring loses relevance. The system begins to recalibrate its baseline, no longer clinging to the older signal. These shifts might not feel dramatic in real time, but their cumulative effect is staggering. You wake up one morning and realize: the old version doesn't feel like "you" anymore.

Still, the initial stage of integration can feel fragile. There's a window of resistance, usually when the excitement fades and the mind tries to conserve energy by returning to old autopilot modes. This is when most people abandon the ritual—not because it wasn't working, but because they didn't *know* that this dip was part of the upgrade. Anticipating this dip allows you to stay conscious through it instead of mistaking it for failure.

At this point, what you need is a stabilizing framework—something that reorients your nervous system and reminds it what it's working toward. Not through willpower, but through pattern-locking.

One of the most effective ways to lock in that pattern is through what might be called anchoring loops. These are short, emotionally charged actions tied to a specific emotional state or identity shift. When done consistently, they create a neurological shortcut. Over time, simply performing the action brings the emotional state online without effort. It becomes an access key to the version of you that originally performed it with intention.

This is the secret to keeping a transformation alive. Most people believe they need to constantly chase motivation or clarity. In truth, they only need to *trigger a known state* that already carries their preferred emotional chemistry. When the body and brain have rehearsed that state often enough, it doesn't need thinking. It needs remembering.

This remembering must be built into the fabric of your days. If you separate your transformation from your environment, your environment will always win. This is why people feel powerful at retreats and lost when they return home. The outer world is filled with cues—subtle signals, associations, sensory imprints—that either reinforce or dissolve what you're becoming. Unless you deliberately shift those cues, your surroundings will unconsciously pull you back.

That's why integration rituals must not be treated as isolated practices, but as *deliberate implants* into your daily rhythm. They must touch the parts of your life you used to leave unconscious: how you wake up, how you enter a room, how you respond to a delay, how you transition between tasks. Each of these moments is programmable. And each one becomes an opportunity to broadcast a new energetic signal.

It helps to think in terms of symbolic acts. These are not performative or aesthetic. They are strategic. A cold shower taken with intention becomes more than hygiene. It becomes a message to the nervous system: we adapt, we choose discomfort, we complete cycles. Closing your laptop at the exact same hour each evening becomes a ritual of energetic sovereignty: this is the boundary, this is the moment I return to self.

Even something as simple as placing your hand over your heart while speaking a phrase can condition the body to associate words with emotion, breath with presence, movement with authority. Repetition makes it real. Emotional charge makes it powerful. Intentional placement into daily flow makes it last.

The key is not perfection. The key is **continuity**. Missing a ritual one day will not erase its effect. What matters is returning. The nervous system does not require flawlessness to build new identity structures. It requires consistency in direction. Even small daily efforts signal your intent to stabilize. And that signal is what gets amplified.

There will be moments when the ritual feels flat, mechanical, or even pointless. This is not failure. This is recalibration. Your system is deciding whether to make it permanent. The power is in your response. Do you reinforce the signal, or do you interpret the dullness as a sign to stop? If you continue, even without the feeling, the ritual becomes stronger. Feeling eventually returns. And when it does, it lands deeper.

True integration is not about doing more. It's about making what you do *unmissable*. A few deliberate signals, repeated with intention and mapped to identity, have more long-term impact than dozens of disconnected practices done without presence. This is the architecture of transformation. Not grand gestures, but subtle imprints. Not chasing change, but embodying decision.

What you repeat becomes your frequency. What you ritualize becomes your reality. The version of you that lives inside your rituals is the version that eventually becomes permanent. Not by force, not by effort, but by design.

Repeating the Protocol at Higher Levels

Transformation is not a one-time event. It is a recursive process, and that process is layered. What works at one level of identity must be reengaged and recalibrated as you evolve. This is where most people fall into the trap of regression—not because the tools stopped working, but because they assumed they wouldn't need to work them again.

The protocol you've been using is not just a method for getting unstuck. It's a blueprint for recalibration, and it's designed to be repeated. But as your baseline state changes, the same tools must be used differently. The version of you who began this journey was likely motivated by discomfort. The version of you reading this now is no longer simply trying to escape. You are trying to expand. That distinction changes everything.

At higher levels, the resistance is subtler. The sabotage wears more sophisticated masks. The loops are not always destructive, but they can still be limiting. You no longer need to override despair. You need to override comfort. You're no longer stuck in pain—you're stuck in identity. And that identity may appear evolved, healed, capable. But it is still a container. And if it isn't consciously upgraded, it becomes a ceiling.

This is where repeating the protocol becomes essential. The same sequence—disruption, reprogramming, embodiment, stabilization—still applies. But your inputs must be sharper, your self-honesty more precise, your calibration tighter. You can't rely on the same emotional leverage. You need to access new levels of clarity, new demands, new visions that challenge even your upgraded self.

That means asking new questions, not just reinforcing old answers. What loop am I in now that feels successful but is actually keeping me small? What identity am I defending with subtle patterns of avoidance or over-control? What version of the future am I resisting because it would require giving up the rewards of who I've already become?

The higher you go, the more tempting it is to rest. Your environment reflects your progress, people affirm your growth, outcomes improve. But the deeper currents of your nervous system can still default to survival mechanisms, only now in more socially acceptable ways. Control replaces chaos. Numbness disguises as calm. Achievement distracts from alignment. The rituals still work, but you begin to treat them like maintenance rather than portals.

To repeat the protocol at this stage, you must re-ignite intention. Not to fix, but to ascend. The nervous system does not automatically evolve just because your circumstances have. It must be led. It must be shown the signal of upgrade through deliberate shifts in perception, energy, and choice. This is not about pushing harder. It's about refining the code.

That refinement begins with your **attention**. The nervous system responds most strongly to what you emotionally emphasize. When you upgrade what you focus on—not just what you want to avoid, but what you now want to become—you create a new signal that reorients your internal architecture.

That new signal must be consistently embedded. The difference now is not just in strength but in precision. At earlier stages, you were learning how to stop reacting and reclaim agency. Now, you are learning how to fine-tune your perception so it only admits what matches your elevated trajectory. You are training the system to become intolerant of anything less than alignment—not through force, but through refinement.

This is where most people unconsciously stall. The protocol has worked. Life has improved. The nervous system settles. But without new inputs, it stabilizes at that level. And that stabilization, while comfortable, becomes a plateau. This is not because growth has stopped, but because it was never designed to be passive. The moment you stop actively shaping the signal, you become shaped by your current environment, even if it's one you once fought hard to create.

To break this loop, you don't need more intensity. You need higher-resolution intention. Ask yourself not what's wrong, but what is no longer enough. Not what hurts, but what no longer excites. Not what's blocking you, but what you're silently tolerating. These are the questions that trigger the next layer of protocol activation.

Every phase of evolution requires a new container. That includes a new emotional language, new rituals of embodiment, and new demands placed on your system. These demands don't come from pressure. They come from decision. Deciding to perceive, feel, and respond as the next version of yourself—not when things get bad, but when everything still seems fine. Especially then.

Your system, once trained, becomes incredibly responsive to subtle cues. That sensitivity must be honored. What you once could ignore—minor inconsistencies, vague tolerations, energy leaks—now require surgical precision. A small misalignment at this level creates ripple effects that pull you back into loops disguised as stability. This is not paranoia. It's mastery. Mastery is not just about control. It's about subtlety. You must become fluent in the smallest shifts within yourself.

The repeated protocol becomes a recalibration ritual. You no longer need it to drag you out of dysfunction. You need it to keep you vibrating at the edge of your next identity. The nervous system loves rhythm. When that rhythm is intentional, it accelerates embodiment. When it's unconscious, it fossilizes the past.

There will be moments where everything inside you resists that next turn of the spiral. Not because it's wrong, but because it threatens the rewards of the current self. This is where protocol repetition becomes non-negotiable. You are not doing it to fix anything. You are doing it to remain loyal to your evolution.

And this loyalty is not about perfection. It's about alignment. The protocol works because it keeps reminding your system what truth feels like. When that truth changes shape, the ritual must evolve too. The nervous system does not care about your goals. It cares about what you consistently feel. It listens to emotional repetition, not logic. So give it new emotions to echo. Give it new truths to reinforce. Give it new edges to normalize.

You are no longer building the structure. You are refining the instrument. And every time you run the protocol again, you tune yourself closer to that highest signal. At this level, repetition is not redundancy. It is revelation.

Printed in Dunstable, United Kingdom

71293970R00080